THE RECTORY CHILDREN

MORE WILDSIDE CLASSICS

Dacobra, or The White Priests of Ahriman, by Harris Burland
The Nabob, by Alphonse Daudet
Out of the Wreck, by Captain A. E. Dingle
The Elm-Tree on the Mall, by Anatole France
The Lance of Kanana, by Harry W. French
Amazon Nights, by Arthur O. Friel
Caught in the Net, by Emile Gaboriau
The Gentle Grafter, by O. Henry
Raffles, by E. W. Hornung
Gates of Empire, by Robert E. Howard
Tom Brown's School Days, by Thomas Hughes
The Opium Ship, by H. Bedford Jones
The Miracles of Antichrist, by Selma Lagerlof
Arsène Lupin, by Maurice LeBlanc
A Phantom Lover, by Vernon Lee
The Iron Heel, by Jack London
The Witness for the Defence, by A.E.W. Mason
The Spider Strain and Other Tales, by Johnston McCulley
Tales of Thubway Tham, by Johnston McCulley
The Prince of Graustark, by George McCutcheon
Bull-Dog Drummond, by Cyril McNeile
The Moon Pool, by A. Merritt
The Red House Mystery, by A. A. Milne
Blix, by Frank Norris
Wings over Tomorrow, by Philip Francis Nowlan
The Devil's Paw, by E. Phillips Oppenheim
Satan's Daughter and Other Tales, by E. Hoffmann Price
The Insidious Dr. Fu Manchu, by Sax Rohmer
Mauprat, by George Sand
The Slayer and Other Tales, by H. de Vere Stacpoole
Penrod (Gordon Grant Illustrated Edition), by Booth Tarkington
The Gilded Age, by Mark Twain
The Blockade Runners, by Jules Verne
The Gadfly, by E.L. Voynich

Please see www.wildsidepress.com for a complete list!

THE RECTORY CHILDREN

MRS MOLESWORTH

WILDSIDE PRESS

THE RECTORY CHILDREN

This edition published in 2006 by Wildside Press, LLC.
www.wildsidepress.com

*'O little hearts! that throb and beat,
With such impatient, feverish heat,
Such limitless and strong desires.'* — Longfellow.

CHAPTER I

THE PARLOUR BEHIND THE SHOP

'I was very solitary indeed.'
(*Visit to the Cousins*). — Mary Lamb.

The blinds had been drawn down for some time in the back parlour behind Mr. Fairchild's shop in Pier Street, the principal street in the little town of Seacove. And the gas was lighted, though it was not turned up very high. It was a great thing to have gas; it had not been known at Seacove till recently. For the time of which I am writing is now a good many years ago, thirty or forty at least.

Seacove, though a small place, was not so out-of-the-way in some respects as many actually larger towns, for it was a seaport, though not a very important one. Ships came in from all parts of the globe, and sailed away again in due course to the far north, and still farther off south; to the great other world of America, too, no doubt, and to the ancient eastern lands. But it was the vessels going to or coming from the strange mysterious north — the land of everlasting snow, where the reindeer and, farther north still, the white bear have their home, and where the winter is one long, long night — it was somehow the thought of the north that had the most fascination for the little girl who was sitting alone in the dull parlour behind the shop this late November evening. And among the queer outlandish-looking sailors who from time to time were to be seen on the wharf or about the Seacove streets, now and then looking in to buy a sheet of paper and an envelope in her father's shop, it was the English ones belonging to the whalers or to the herring smacks bound for the north who interested Celestina by far the most.

This evening she was not thinking of sailors or ships or anything like that; her mind was full of her own small affairs. She had got two new dolls, quite tiny ones — Celestina did not care for big dolls — and long as the daylight lasted she had been perfectly happy dressing them. But the daylight was gone now — it was always rather in a hurry to say good-night to the back parlour — and the gas was too dim for her to see clearly by, even if she had

had anything else to do, which she had not, till mother could give her a scrap or two for the second dolly's frock. It was mother she was longing for. She wanted to show her the hats and cloaks she had made out of some tiny bits for both the dollies — the cloaks, that is to say, for the hats were crochet-work, crocheted in pink cotton. Celestina's little fingers were very clever at crochet.

'Oh, mother, mother,' she said half aloud, '*do* come.'

She had drawn back the little green baize curtain which hung before the small window between the shop and the parlour, and was peering in, her nose flattened against the glass. She was allowed to do this, but she was not allowed to run out and in of the shop without leave, and at this time of the day, or evening, even when there were few customers, she knew that her father and mother were generally busy. There were late parcels to put up for the little errand-boy to leave on his way home; there was the shop to tidy, and always a good many entries to make in the big ledger. Very often there were letters to write and send off, ordering supplies needed for the shop, or books not in stock, which some customer had asked for.

It was a bookseller's and stationer's shop; the only one worthy of the name at Seacove. And Mr. Fairchild did a pretty good business, though certainly, as far as the actual *book* part of it was concerned, people read and bought far fewer books thirty years ago than now. And books were much dearer. People wrote fewer letters too; paper and envelopes were dearer also. Still, one way and another it was not a bad business of its kind in a modest way, though strict economy and care were required to make a livelihood out of it. And some things had made this more difficult than would otherwise have been the case. Delicate health perhaps most of all. Mr. Fairchild was not very strong, and little Celestina had been fragile enough as a baby and a tiny girl, though now she was growing stronger. No wonder that a great share of both work and care fell on Celestina's mother, and this the little girl already understood, and tried always to remember.

But it was dull and lonely sometimes. She had few companions, and for some months past she had not gone to school, as a rather serious illness had made her unable to go out in bad weather. She did not mind this much; she liked to do lessons by herself, for father or mother to correct when they had time, and there was no child at school she cared for particularly. Still poor Celestina was pining for companionship without knowing it. Perhaps, though mother said little, she understood more about it than appeared.

And 'Oh, mother, mother, *do* come,' the child repeated, as she peered through the glass.

There were one or two customers in the shop still. One of them Celestina knew by sight. It was Mr. Redding, the organist of the church. He was choosing some music-paper, and talking as he did so, but the pair of ears behind the window could not hear what he said, though by his manner it seemed something not only of interest to himself but to his hearers also.

'I wish I could hear what he's saying,' thought the little maiden, 'or most of all, I *wish* he'd go and that other man too — oh, he's going, but Mr. Redding is asking for something else now! Oh, if only mother would come, or if I might turn on the gas higher. I think it would be nicer to have candles, like Fanny Wells has in her house. Gas is only nice when it's very high turned on, and mother says it costs such a lot then. I *do* so want to show mother the cloaks and hats.'

She turned back at last, wearied of waiting and watching. The fire was burning brightly, that was some comfort, and Celestina sat down on the rug in front of it, propping her two little dolls against the fender.

'Tomorrow,' she said to herself, 'as soon as I've made a frock for Eleanor, I'll have a tea-party. Eleanor and Amy shall be new friends coming to tea for the first time — if *only* the parlour chairs weren't too big for the table!' she sighed deeply. 'They can't look nice and *real*, when they're so high up that their legs won't go underneath. People don't make our tables and chairs like that — I don't see why they can't make doll-house ones properly. Now, if I was a carpenter I'd make a doll-house just like a real house — I could make it so nice.'

She began building doll-houses — her favourite castles in the air — in imagination. But now and then she wanted another opinion, there were knotty points to decide. As 'all roads,' according to the old proverb, 'lead to Rome,' so all Celestina's meditations ended in the old cry, 'If only mother would come.'

The door opened at last — gently, so gently that the little girl knew it could be no one else but mother. She sprang up.

'Oh, mother, I am so glad you've come. I've been so tired waiting. I do so want to show you the cloaks and hats, and *can* you give me a bit to make Amy's frock? She looks so funny with a cloak and hat and no frock.'

'I will try to find you a scrap of something when I go upstairs,' mother replied. 'But just now I must see about getting tea ready. Father is tired already, and he has a good deal to do this evening still. Yes, you have made the cloaks very nice, and the little hats too. I'll turn up the gas so as to see better.'

Celestina gave in without a murmur to waiting till after tea for the piece of stuff she longed for so ardently, and she set to work in a neat, handy way to help her mother with the tea-table. They understood each other perfectly, these two, though few words of endearment passed between them, and caresses were rare. People were somewhat colder in manner at that time than nowadays perhaps; much petting of children was not thought good for them, and especially in the case of an only child, parents had great fear of 'spoiling.' But no one who looked at Mrs. Fairchild's sweet face as her eyes rested lovingly on her little girl could have doubted for a moment her intense affection. She had a very sweet face; Celestina thought there never could be anybody prettier than mother, and I don't know that she was far wrong. If she ever thought of herself at all — of her looks especially — it was to hope that some day she might grow up to be 'like mother.'

Tea was ready — neatly arranged on the table, though all was of the plainest, a little carefully-made toast to tempt father's uncertain appetite the only approach to luxury — when Mr. Fairchild came in and sat down in the one arm-chair rather wearily. He was a tall thin man, and he stooped a good deal. He had a kindly though rather nervous and careworn face and bright intelligent eyes.

'Redding is full of news as usual,' he said, as Mrs. Fairchild handed him his tea. 'He is a good-natured man, but I wish he wouldn't talk quite so much.'

'He had some excuse for talking this evening,' said Celestina's mother; 'it is news of importance for every one at Seacove, and of course it must affect Mr. Redding a good deal. I shall be glad if the new clergyman is more hearty about improving the music.'

Celestina so far had heard without taking in the drift of the conversation, but at the last words she pricked up her ears.

'Is there going to be a new clergyman — is old Dr. Bunton going away, mother?' she asked eagerly, though the moment after she reddened slightly, not at all sure that she was not going to be told that 'little girls should not ask questions.' But both Mr. and Mrs. Fairchild were interested in the subject — I think for once they forgot that Celestina was only 'a little girl.'

'Yes,' the mother replied; 'he is giving up at last. That has been known for some weeks, but it is only today that it has been known who is to succeed him. Mr. Vane, that is the name, is it not?' she added, turning to her husband.

'The Reverend Bernard Vane, at present vicar of St. Cyprian's, somewhere in the west end of London — that is Redding's description of him,' Mr. Fairchild replied. 'I don't know how a fashionable London clergyman will settle down at Seacove, nor what his reasons are for coming here, I'm sure. I hope the change will be for good.'

But his tone showed that he was not at all certain that it would prove so.

'Is he married?' asked Celestina's mother. 'Oh yes, by the bye, I remember Mr. Redding spoke of children, but old Captain Deal came in just as he was telling more and I could not hear the rest.'

'There are several children and Mrs. Vane a youngish lady still, he said. The old Rectory will want some overhauling before they come to it, I should say,' remarked Mr. Fairchild. 'It must be nigh upon forty years since Dr. Bunton came there, and there's not much been done in the way of repairs, save a little whitewashing now and then. The doctor and Mrs. Bunton haven't needed much just by themselves — but a family's different; they'll be needing nurseries and schoolrooms and what not, especially if they have been used to grand London ways.'

Celestina had been turning her bright brown eyes from one parent to another in turn as they spoke.

'Is London much grander than Seacove?' she asked. 'I thought the Rectory was such a fine house.'

Mrs. Fairchild smiled.

'It might be made very nice. There's plenty of room any way. And many clergymen's families are very simple and homely.'

'I wonder if there are any little girls,' said Celestina. 'And do you think they'll go to Miss Peters's to school, mother?'

Her father turned on her rather sharply.

'Dear me, no, child. Of course not,' he said. 'Miss Peters's is well enough for plain Seacove folk, but don't you be getting any nonsense in your head of setting up to be the same as ladies' children. Mrs. Vane comes of a high family, I hear; there will be a French ma'amselle of a governess as like as not.'

Celestina looked at her father with a world of puzzle in her eyes, her little pale face with a red spot of excitement on each cheek. But she was not the least hurt by her father's words. She simply did not understand them: what are called 'class distinctions' were quite unknown to her innocent mind. Had she been alone with her mother she might have asked for some explanation, but she was too much in awe of her father to question him.

Her mother turned to her somewhat abruptly.

'I want some more water; the kettle, Celestina love,' she said; and as the little girl brought it, 'I will explain to you afterwards, but don't say any more. Father is tired,' she whispered.

And Celestina quickly forgot all about it; the sight of Eleanor and Amy still reposing on the hearthrug as she replaced the kettle drove out of her mind all thoughts of the possible little Misses Vane.

After tea, when the things were cleared away and Celestina had helped her mother to make the room look neat and comfortable again, fox the little servant in the kitchen was seldom seen in the parlour, as she fidgeted Mr. Fairchild by her awkward clattering ways, Mrs. Fairchild went upstairs to fetch some sewing that needed seeing to.

'I will look for a scrap or two for you,' she said to Celestina as she went. 'But I'm not sure that you should sew any more tonight. It's trying for your eyes.'

'And what about your sums, child?' said her father. 'Have you done all I set you?'

'Yes, father, and I've read the chapter of *Little Arthur's History* too,' Celestina replied.

'Well, then,' said Mr. Fairchild, drawing his chair nearer to the table again — he had pushed it close to the fire — 'bring your slate and your books. I'll correct the sums and set you some more, and then we'll have a little history. I will question you first on the chapter you have read to yourself.'

Celestina could not help an appealing glance at her mother — she had the two little dolls in her hand, poor Amy still looking very deplorable in her skirt-less condition. Mrs. Fairchild understood her though no word was spoken.

'I thought you were going back to write in the shop,' she said gently to her husband. 'The stove is still hot.'

'I am too tired,' he replied, and indeed he looked so. 'There is nothing so very pressing, and it's too late for the London post. No — I would rather take Celly's lessons; it will be a change.'

Mrs. Fairchild said no more, nor did Celestina — father's word was law. The little girl did not even look cross or doleful, though she gave a tiny sigh as she fetched her books. She was a docile pupil, thoughtful and attentive, though not peculiarly quick, and Mr. Fairchild, in spite of his rather nervously irritable temper, was an earnest and intelligent teacher. The sums were fairly correct and the multiplication table was repeated faultlessly. But when it came to the history Celestina was less ready and accurate in her replies.

'My dear,' said her mother, who had sat down beside them with her sewing by this time, 'you are not giving your full attention. I can see you are thinking of something else. If it is anything you do not understand ask father to explain it.'

'Certainly,' Mr. Fairchild agreed. 'There is nothing worse than giving half attention. What are you thinking about, child?'

Celestina looked up timidly.

'It wasn't anything in the lesson — at least not exactly,' she said. 'But when father asked me who was the king of France then, it made me think of what father said about a French ma'amselle, and I wondered what it meant.'

'Ma'amselle,' said her father, 'is only our English way of saying "mademoiselle," which means a miss, a young lady.'

'But those young ladies, the Rectory young ladies, aren't French,' Celestina said.

'Of course not. What I meant was that very likely they have a French governess. It's the mode nowadays when every one wants to speak French well.'

'Oh,' said Celestina, 'I didn't understand. I'd like to hear somebody speak French,' she added. 'Did you ever hear it, mother?'

'Yes,' Mrs. Fairchild replied. 'When I was a girl there was a French lady came to live near us that I was very fond of; and she was very kind to us. She sent me a beautiful present when I married. I called you after her, you know, Celestina — I'm sure I've told you that before. Her name was Célestine.'

'I remember,' the little girl replied; 'but I forgot about her being French. I would like to see her, mother.'

'I do not know if she is still alive,' said Mrs. Fairchild. 'She must be an old lady by now, if so. She went back to France many years ago; she was in England with her husband, who had some business here. They had no children, and she was always asking mother to let her adopt me. But though there were so many of us, mother couldn't make up her mind to spare one.'

'Things would have turned out pretty different for you, Mary, if she had. You'd have been married to a French "mounseer" by now,' and he laughed a little, as if there was something exceedingly funny in the idea. Mr. Fairchild did not often laugh.

'Maybe,' his wife replied, smiling.

'I do hope they'll have a French governess,' said Celestina.

'Who? oh, the Miss Vanes,' said her father. 'Why, you *are* putting the cart before the horse, child! We don't even know that the new clergyman has any daughters — his family may be all boys. Besides, I don't know when you'd be likely to see them or their governess either.'

'They'd be sure to come to the shop sometimes, father,' Celestina replied eagerly. 'Even old Mrs. Bunton does — I've often seen her. And there's no other shop for books and stationery at Seacove.'

Mr. Fairchild smiled at the pride with which she said this.

'It would be a bad job for me if there were,' he said, 'for as it is there's barely custom for a shop of the kind,' and an anxious look came over his face. But Mrs. Fairchild reminded him that if they did not finish the chapter of *Little Arthur* quickly, it would be Celestina's bedtime, so the talk changed to the Black Prince and his exploits.

CHAPTER II

THOSE YOUNG LADIES

> 'Leave me alone — I want to cry;
> It's no use trying to be good.' — Anon.

Six weeks or so later — Christmas and New Year's day were past; it was the middle of January by this time — a little group of children might have been seen standing on the shore about half a mile from Seacove.

Though midwinter, it was not very cold. There is a theory that it never is very cold at the seaside. I cannot say that I have always found this the case, but it was so at Seacove. It lay in a sheltered position, out of the way of the east wind, and this was one reason why Mr. Vane had decided to make it for a time the home of himself and his family.

These were his children — the group on the seashore. Rumour had exaggerated a little in saying he had 'several.' There were but three of them, and of these three two were girls. So Celestina Fairchild's thoughts about them had some foundation after all.

'It looks just a little, a very little dreary,' said the eldest of the three, a girl of thirteen or so, slight and rather tall for her age, with a pretty graceful figure and pretty delicate features; 'but then of course it's the middle of winter. Not that spring or summer would make much difference here; there are so very few trees.'

She glanced round her as she spoke. It was a bare, almost desolate-looking stretch of country, down to the sea, which was still and gray-looking this morning. Yet there was a strange charm about it too — the land, though by no means hilly, was undulating. Not far from where the children stood there was a grand run of sand-hills, with coarse, strong grass and a few hardy thistles, and, in its season, bindweed with its white and pinky flowers, growing along their summit. Farther off was a sort of skeleton-like erection, looking not unlike the gaunt remains of a deserted sail-less ship: this was a landmark or beacon, placed there to point out a sudden turn in the coastline. And out at sea, a mile or so distant, stood a lighthouse with a revolving lantern; three times in each minute the bright light was to be seen as soon as night fell. A kind of natural breakwater ran out in a straight line to the lighthouse, so that in low tides — and the tides are sometimes very low at Seacove — it was difficult to believe but that you could get on foot all the way to the lighthouse rock.

But all these interesting particulars were not as yet known to Mr. Vane's children. They had arrived at Seacove Rectory only the night before.

The boy — he was next in age to his elder sister Rosalys — followed the direction of her glance.

'No,' he said, 'there's very few trees, certainly. But I think it's going to be very jolly all the same. When I get my pony *I'll* be all right any way; and on Saturdays, or odd half-holidays — there always are odd half-holidays at every school, you know — I'll take you girls out a drive in that funny little donkey-chaise, or whatever it is, that's standing in the coach-house.'

'I don't fancy there are many places to drive to,' Rosalys replied. 'Papa said there would be no use in having any sort of proper carriage. The only good road is the one to your school, Rough, and you'll have enough of that morning and evening.'

'Papa said Seacove was a — I can't remember the word — something French — cool — cul — '

'*Cul-de-sac*,' said Rosalys; 'leading to nowhere, that means.'

'Except to the sea, I suppose,' added the little girl who had stumbled at the French word. 'It would be nice to have a ship of our own instead of a carriage. Don't you think we might ask papa to get us one?'

'A *ship*, Biddy — I suppose you mean a boat,' said Rosalys, in a rather 'superior' tone. 'No; I don't fancy papa would trust us to go about in a boat. Mamma would be frightened out of her wits about us.'

'The sea looks *so* quiet,' said Bridget, gazing out at it. 'I don't think it could ever be tossy and soapy here like it used to be at Rockcliffe.'

'Couldn't it just?' said Randolph. 'Wait a bit, Bride. It may look quiet on a day like this, and inside the shelter of the bay, but I can tell you there's jolly rough work outside there sometimes. I was talking to an old sailor this morning when I ran out before breakfast.'

'I'd like to see a shipwreck — I mean,' as she caught sight of a shocked expression on her sister's face — 'I mean of course one that nobody would be drowned in.'

'But how could any one be sure of that? You should be more careful what you say, Bride; you are so heedless.'

Bridget's face puckered up. It was rather given to puckering up, funny little face that it was. She was eight years old, short and rather stout, with thick, dark hair and a freckled complexion. Her nose turned up and her mouth was not small. But she was not ugly; she had merry gray eyes and very white teeth. Somehow, thorough little English girl though she was, she reminded one of the small Savoyard boys one sees with a box of marmots slung in front of them, or a barrel organ and a monkey.

'I didn't mean to say anything naughty, Alie,' she began, in a plaintive tone. 'I'm always — '

'Oh, come now, Biddy, stop that, do,' said her brother; 'don't spoil the first morning by going off into a howl for nothing. No one supposes you wanted to drown a lot of people for the sake of watching a shipwreck, only, as Alie says, you should be more careful. Strangers might think you a very queer little girl if they heard you say such a thing.'

Bridget still looked melancholy, but she did not venture to complain any more. She was a good deal in awe of Rough, who was twelve and a big boy for his age. He had been at school for two years, and now he was going as a day-scholar to a large and very excellent public school, which was only about two miles from Seacove, quite in the country. Mr. Vane had bought a pony for him to ride backwards and forwards, so Randolph was in capital spirits. But he was not an unkind or selfish boy, and though his pet name 'Rough' suited him sometimes as regarded his manners, his heart was gentle. And indeed the name had been given to him at first on account of his thick shaggy hair, as a very little boy.

'It's rather cold standing about,' said Rosalys. 'Don't you think we'd better walk on or take a run?'

'Let's have a race,' said Rough. 'The sand's nice and firm about here. I'll give you a good start, Alie, and Biddy can run on in front and wait till we call to her that we're off.'

Bridget trotted off as she was told, obediently. She did not care much for running. Her legs were short and she was rather fat, but she did not like to complain. She ran on, though slowly, till at last Randolph shouted to her to stop. Then she stood still waiting till he called to her again, for he and Rosalys took some time to settle how much of a start Alie was to have — from where she stood, Biddy heard them talking and measuring.

'I wish they wouldn't run races,' thought the little girl. 'They're so big compared with me — they've such much longer legs. I shan't like Seacove if they're going always to run races. In London they couldn't in the streets; it was only when we went in the gardens, and that wasn't every day, it was too far to go. I wish I had a brother or a sister littler than me; it's too much difference between Alie and me, thirteen and eight. I wish — '

But here came a whoop from behind.

'Off, Biddy; look sharp — one, two, three.'

Poor Biddy — off she set as fast as she *could* go, which is not saying much. She puffed and panted, for she was not without a spirit of her own and did not want to be overtaken *too* soon. And for a time Rough's cries of encouragement, 'Gee-up, old woman,' 'Famous, Biddy,' 'You'll win yet,' and so on, spurred her to fresh exertions. But not for long; she felt her powers flagging, and as first Alie and then Rough, both apparently as fresh as ever, passed her at full speed, she gave in.

'It's no use. I can't run races. I wish you wouldn't make me,' she said, as in a minute or two the two others came flying back again to where she stood, a convenient goal for their return race.

'But you ran splendidly for a bit,' said Randolph; 'and I'll tell you what, Biddy, it would be a very good thing for you to run a good deal more than you do. It'll make you grow and stop you getting too fat.'

'I'm not fatter than you were when you were as little as me, Roughie. Nurse says so — you were a regular roundabout till you had the measles; mamma says so too,' replied Bridget philosophically.

'I'm quite hot,' said Rosalys; 'fancy being hot in January! But we'd better not stand still or we'll get a chill. Isn't it nice to come out alone? I'd like to walk to Seacove — I want to see what it's like, but of course we mustn't go so far. Mamma said we must stay on the shore.'

'If it was summer we might dig and make sand-castles,' said Biddy regretfully. Digging in the sand was an amusement much more to her taste than running races.

'I think that's stupid — it's such baby play,' Rosalys replied. 'But come on, do. I'm going to climb up to the top of that bank — that's the sand-hills papa was speaking about.'

It was more tiring work than she had expected. Before they got to the top of the bank Alie had decided that they would have done better to remain where they were, on the smooth firm sand down below, but once at the top she changed again. What fun can be more delightful than playing in sand-hills, jumping from a miniature summit to the valley beneath with no fear of hurting one's self even if one comes to grief and rolls ignominiously as far as one can go! How helplessly one wades in the shifting, unstable footing — tumbling over with a touch, like a house built of cards! The children's laughter sounded merrily in the clear cold air; Bridget plunged about like a little porpoise in the water, and Rosalys quite forgot that she had attained the dignity of her teens.

But a bell ringing suddenly some little way off caught their ears.

'That's papa ringing,' said Randolph. 'He said he'd have the big dinner-bell rung when it was time for me to go in. I'm going to walk to the town or the village, or whatever it is, with him. Good-bye, girls. It's only three o'clock — you can stay another half-hour,' and off he ran.

'Let's go down to the shore again,' said Alie. 'Mamma said *perhaps* she'd come out a little, and she'd never see us up here.'

Bridget hung back a little.

'I daresay she won't come out,' she said. 'Do stay up here, Alie. If mamma comes out she'll only talk to you and I'll be all alone. I don't want her.'

'Oh, Bride, that's not nice. I'm sure mamma likes to talk to you too, only you see I'm older, and there's often things you wouldn't understand about perhaps, and — '

'I know — it's always the same. I'm too little to be any use. I know you're older and sensibler, and I don't mean that mamma's not kind. But families should be settled better — and — oh, Alie, I have so torn my frock, and it's my afternoon one — my new merino.'

Rosalys looked much concerned.

'*What* a pity!' she exclaimed. 'I wish we hadn't played in the sand. But really, Biddy, you are very unlucky. I've been jumping just as much as you, and I've got no harm.'

'You never do — I don't know how it is that I always get torn,' said Bride dolefully. 'And oh, Alie, there is mamma' — they were down on the shore by this time, coming down being a much speedier affair than climbing up, — 'she will be so vexed, for I've got this frock new, extra to yours, you know, because of the stain on the other the day I spilt my tea all down it. I am so sorry, Alie. Could you pin it up?'

Rosalys stooped to examine the damage. It was not *very* great, still under the circumstances of its being a new frock, it was vexing enough.

'You've got it so sandy, too — that makes it look worse,' said the elder sister, giving the unlucky skirt a shake as she spoke.

'I wish mamma hadn't come out,' said Bridget. 'Then I could have got it brushed and mended before I told her, but perhaps it's best to tell at once,' and she gave a little sigh.

'Much best,' her sister agreed, and they went on to meet their mother. Suddenly Bride gave a little cry of satisfaction.

'Oh, Smut's with mamma,' she exclaimed. 'I'm so glad. You can walk with mamma alone then, Alie, and Smut and I will come after you. I'm always quite happy with Smuttie — I wish he was my very own.'

It was rather unlucky that just as they got up to Mrs. Vane, Bridget was so occupied in calling to Smut, who came careering forward to meet the girls, that the dilapidated frock went quite out of her mind. At the first moment her mother did not notice it.

'Well, dears, here I am!' she began brightly. 'I got my letters finished more quickly than I expected. What a quantity of things there are to order when one first comes to a new house! And I do so miss M'Creagh! Did you see me coming, Alie darling?'

'Yes, mamma — not very far off though. We were up on the sand-hills when papa rang for Rough, and — '

But Mrs. Vane interrupted her.

'Oh, Bridget,' she exclaimed in a tone of vexation, 'what have you been doing to yourself? Do you see, Alie? Her skirt is torn from top to bottom — the stuff torn, not the seam. And so dirty. Your new frock too — really, child, you are too provoking.'

Biddy's round rosy face grew longer and redder, and her eyes filled with tears. She opened her mouth to speak, but Rosalys came before her.

'It isn't so very bad, dear mamma,' she said eagerly. 'I've been looking at it. It looks worse because of the sand, but it isn't really dirty; it will brush off. She rolled down one of the sand-hills. I'm afraid it was my fault. It was my idea to play about there.'

Mrs. Vane glanced at Alie's own garments.

'Your frock is none the worse,' she said. 'I do not see that Bride need have hurt hers if she had been the least careful. But you are so incorrigibly heedless, Bridget, and *so* thoughtless. Why, you were dancing and jumping and calling to Smut when I met you as if there was nothing the matter! I suppose you had forgotten all about your frock already.'

Mrs. Vane's voice was rather sharp as she spoke thus to the little girl. It sounded quite differently from the bright sweet tone in which she had greeted them. And it did not seem to suit her to speak sharply. She was very pretty and sweet-looking, and she seemed young to be tall Alie's mother; indeed, people often said they looked more like sisters: stout, sturdy little Bridget was quite unlike them both.

Rosalys looked up at her mother anxiously. She could not bear her to be troubled, and though she was sorry for Bridget, she was vexed with her too. She slipped her arm inside Mrs. Vane's and drew her on.

'It's too cold to stand still, mamma dear,' she said. 'Let us walk on to that beautiful smooth piece of sand — it's rather stony just here. Biddy, take care of Smut.'

That meant, 'You may stay behind and keep out of the way a little.' Biddy had no objection to do so.

'Come, Smuttie, stay by me,' she said coaxingly to the little shaggy black dog. Smut was very fond of Bridget, who had a very big heart for all dumb animals. He wagged his tail and looked up in her face with inquiring sympathy, for he saw quite well that Biddy was in trouble. This was nothing new; many and many a time had the little girl buried her tearful face in his rough coat and sobbed out her sorrows to him. They were never very big sorrows really, but they were big to her, and rendered bigger by the knowledge in her honest little heart that they were generally and mostly, if not entirely, brought about by her own fault.

She could not stoop down to cry on Smut's back now; it would have risked considerable more dirtying of her poor frock. But she stayed some way behind her mother and sister, so that she might talk without being overheard by any one save her four-legged companion.

'Smuttie,' she said, 'I'm very unhappy. This is only the second day at Seacove and I've vexed mamma already. I made good resol — never mind; *you* know what I mean, Smut — to begin new here, and it's all gone. I don't know what to do, Smuttie, I truly don't. Alie means to be kind, but it's quite easy for her to be good, I think. And it's no good me trying. It really isn't, so I think I'll just leave off and be comfortable.'

Smut looked up and wagged his tail. He was quite ready to agree with anything Biddy proposed, so long as she spoke cheerfully and did not cry.

'Good little Smuttie, kind little Smut,' said the child; 'you're so nice and understanding always.'

But Smut seemed restless; he fidgeted about in front of Bride, first running a step or two, then stopping to wag his tail and look back appealingly at her in an insinuating doggy way of his own. Biddy pretended not to know what he meant, but she could not long keep up this feint.

'I do know what you want,' she said at last with a sigh. 'It's a scamper, and I hate running, and I'm sure you know I do. But I suppose I must do it to please you. You won't roar after me like Rough, anyway.'

And off she set, her short legs exerting themselves valiantly for Smuttie's sake. He of course could have run much faster, but he was far too much of a gentleman to do so, and he stayed beside her, contenting himself every now and then by stopping short to look up at her, with a quick cheery bark of satisfaction and encouragement.

CHAPTER III

A TRYING CHILD

> 'I think words are little live creatures,
> A species of mischievous elves.'
> —*Child Nature.*

Bride and Smuttie did not overtake Mrs. Vane and Rosalys, for they were running towards the sea, whereas the others were walking straight along the shore. But the dog's bark and the sound once or twice of the child's voice speaking to him came clearly through the still winter air.

Mrs. Vane stopped for a moment and looked after them. She and Alie had been talking about Bridget as they walked.

'There she is again,' said her mother, 'as merry and thoughtless as can be. That is the worst of her, Alie, you can make no impression on her.'

'I don't think it's quite that, mamma,' Rosalys replied, 'though I know it often seems so. She was really very, very sorry about her frock. And she's so young — she's not eight yet, mamma.'

'You were quite different at eight,' answered Mrs. Vane. 'Just think — that time I was so ill and papa was away. You were barely seven, and what a thoughtful, careful little body you were! I shall never forget waking up early one morning and seeing a little white figure stealthily putting coal on the fire, which was nearly out; taking up the lumps with its own little cold hands not to make a noise. My good little Alie!' and she stroked the hand that lay on her arm fondly.

Rosalys smiled up at her. She loved her mother to speak so to her, but still her heart was sore for Biddy.

'I believe — I *know* Biddy would be just as loving to you, mamma, if she knew how,' she said. 'But it is true that she's very provoking. Perhaps it would be different if she had brothers and sisters younger than herself — then she'd *have* to feel herself big and — as if it mattered what she did.'

'Responsible, you mean,' said Mrs. Vane. 'Yes, that is the best training. But we can't provide small brothers and sisters ready-made for Biddy, and I am very well contented with the three I have got! It might be a good thing if she had some companions nearer her own age, but even that has its difficulties. Just think of the scrapes she got into that time I sent her to your aunt's for a fortnight! Why, she was sent home in disgrace for — what was it for — I forget? Biddy's scrapes are so many.'

'For taking the two smallest children to bathe in the pond before breakfast, wasn't it?' said Alie.

'Oh yes — after having half killed their valuable Persian cat by feeding it with cheese-cakes, or something of the kind,' added Mrs. Vane.

But she could not help smiling a little. Alie had already seen that she was softening; whenever mamma called Bridget 'Biddy,' she knew it was a good sign.

'There is one comfort,' said the elder sister, in her motherly way, 'Biddy has a *terribly* kind heart. She is never naughty out of — out of *naughtiness*. But oh, mamma, let us wait a minute; the sunset is beginning.'

And so indeed it was. Over there — far out, over the western sea, the cold, quiet, winter sea, the sun was growing red as he slowly sank, till he seemed to kiss the ocean, which glowed, blushing, in return. It was all red and gray tonight — red and gray only, though there were grandly splendid sunsets at Seacove sometimes, when every shade and colour which light can show to our eyes shone out as if a veil were drawn back from the mysterious glory we may but glimpse at. But the red and gray were very beautiful in their way, and the unusual stillness, broken only by the soft monotonous lap, lap, of the wavelets as they rippled themselves into nothing on the sand, seemed to suit the gentle tones of the sky. And some way off, nearer the sea, seeming farther away than they really were, as they stood right in the ruddy trail of light, were two little figures, both looking black by contrast, though in point of fact only one was so. They were Bridget and Smut, both apparently absorbed in admiring the sunset.

'Isn't it beautiful, Smuttie?' Biddy was saying. 'It's the sun going to bed, you know, dear.'

Smut wagged his tail.

'It's so pretty,' she continued, 'that it makes me think I'd like to be good. P'raps I'd better fix to try again after all — what do you think, Smut?'

Repeated and more energetic tail-wagging, accompanied this time by a short sharp bark. Smut has had enough of the sunset and standing still; he wants to be off again. But Bride interprets his response in her own way.

'You think it would be better? — thank you, dear, for saying so. You are so nice, Smut, for always understanding. Well, I will then, and I'll begin by telling mamma I'm dreadfully sorry about my frock. Good-night, sun — I wish I lived out in the lighthouse — one could see the sun right down in the sea out there, I should think. I wonder if he stays in the sea all night till he comes up at the other side in the morning? No — I don't think he can though, for it says in my jography that it's sunshine at the other side of the world when it's night here, so he can't stay in the sea. I must ask Alie — p'raps it's not the same sun as in London.'

She turned, followed by Smut, who, failing to persuade her to another scamper, consoled himself by poking his nose into the sand in search of unknown dainties which I fear were not to be found. The pair came up to Mrs. Vane and Rosalys, who seemed to be waiting for them.

'Mamma,' Biddy began, in a very contrite tone, 'I've been thinking and I want to tell you I am truly and really very, *very* sorry about my frock. I didn't mean not to seem sorry. I can't think how it got torn, for Alie didn't tear hers, and she was playing about just the same.'

'I don't know either, Biddy,' said her mother. 'It is just the old story, you must be more careful. Perhaps, to go back to the beginning, it would have been better to change to an old frock if you meant to romp about; *or*, it would have been better still perhaps, not to romp when you knew you had a good frock on.'

'That was my fault, mamma,' Alie put in.

'Well, we must try and get the mischief repaired, and let us hope it will be a reminder to you, Biddy, every time you wear this frock.'

Bridget murmured something; she meant to be very good. But when she got a little behind her mother and Alie again she gave herself a shake.

'I shouldn't like that at all,' she thought. 'I should hate this frock if it was always to remind me. I think mamma is rather like the mamma in *Rosamund* when she speaks that way, and I'm like Rosamund on her day of misfortunes, only all my days are days of misfortunes. But I do think I'm nicer than she was.'

As they reached the edge of the shore, where a gate opened into a pathway through a field to the Rectory itself, Mrs. Vane stopped to look across once more at the sunset.

'Yes, he is just going — just. Look, children.'

Alie turned too, but Biddy walked on.

'I don't want to look again,' she said. 'I've said good-night to him once.'

Mrs. Vane glanced at Rosalys.

'What's the matter now?' her glance seemed to say.

Rosalys smiled back.

'It isn't naughtiness,' she whispered. 'It's only some fancy.'

And so it was.

'I said good-night to him when I'd fixed to try to be good,' Bride was saying to herself, 'and if I look at him again now it'll undo the fixing. Besides, I've begun to feel a little naughty again already — I don't like Rosamund's mamma.'

As they walked up the path, Smut, who was really Mrs. Vane's dog and had got his own ideas as to etiquette, returned to his mistress's side and trotted along gravely. He knew that his chances of scampers were over for the day, for not even the most ardent runner could have crossed the field at full speed without coming to grief. It was rough and stony, and to call it a field was a figure of speech; the soil was nothing but sand, and the grass was of the coarsest. But the Rectory stood on rather rising ground, and old Dr. Bunton and his wife had fortunately been fond of gardening. The lawn on the farther side of the house was very respectable, and more flowers and shrubs had been coaxed to grow than could have been expected. Still, to newcomers fresh from a comfortable town-house — and there is no denying that as far as comfort goes a town-house in winter has many advantages over a small country one — it did look somewhat dreary and desolate. All the brightness had gone out of the sky by now; it loomed blue-gray behind the chimneys, and a faint murmuring as of wind in the distance getting up its forces began to be heard.

Mrs. Vane shivered a little.

'I do hope your father and Randolph will be in soon,' she said. 'It may be very mild here, but it strikes me as chilly all the same. I really don't think it is wise to stay out so late, and it has been so almost unnaturally still all day, I shouldn't wonder if it was setting in for stormy weather.'

Biddy's eyes sparkled.

'I would so like,' she was beginning, but she suddenly checked herself. 'Are there always shipwrecks when there's storms?' she asked.

'I fear so,' her mother replied.

'Then I mustn't like storms, I suppose,' said the child. 'It's very tiresome — everything's made the wrong way.'

'Bridget, take care what you're saying,' Mrs. Vane said almost sternly.

Biddy's face did not pucker up, but a dark look came over it, taking away all the pleasant brightness and the merry eagerness of the gray eyes. She did not often look like that, fortunately, for it made her almost ugly. And though her face cleared a little after a while, still it was gloomy, like the darkening sky outside, when she followed Alie downstairs to tea, after they had taken off their things and the torn frock had been changed.

Things had hardly got into their regular order yet at Seacove Rectory. The Vanes had only been there three days, and every one knows that the troubles of a removal, especially to a considerable distance, are very much aggravated when it takes place in mid-winter. It was not to be wondered at that 'mamma' felt both tired and rather dispirited. She was a little homesick too, for mammas can feel homesick as well as both boys and girls; and indeed I would not take upon myself to say that 'papas' are quite above this weakness either. Christmas time had been spent at Mrs. Vane's old home, a warm, cheery, old-fashioned country-house, where grandpapa and grandmamma were still hale and hearty, and never so happy as when surrounded by their grandchildren. This old home of mamma's was within easy access of London too; no wonder, therefore, that the remote seaside rectory seemed a kind of exile to Mrs. Vane, though the reasons that had made Mr. Vane accept the offer of Seacove had been very important ones.

Rosalys, and Randolph too, though in a less thoughtful way, understood all this, and both of the elder children were anxious to help and cheer their parents to the best of their ability. And as all children love change, and most children enjoy, for a time at least, the freedom and independence of the country, it was much less trying for them than for their father and mother. To Bridget the idea of coming to live altogether at the seaside was one of unmixed pleasure. She dearly loved the sea, and all she had hitherto known of it was in pleasant summer weather, and at a bright amusing little place called Rockcliffe. Seacove was certainly not exactly what she had expected; still, sand-hills and a great stretch of splendid shore were not to be despised. I feel sure, however, that young as she was she would have sympathised with her mother, and tried 'extra' hard not to vex her, had she known more about it all. But very little had been explained to her; indeed, Rosalys had been forbidden to say much about the reasons for the change to her little sister. 'She is such a baby for her age, and so heedless,' said Mrs. Vane. In treating Bride thus, I think her mother made a mistake.

The children's tea was laid out in the dining-room, for the schoolroom was still in a chaotic state, and Miss Millet, the governess, was not coming back for another week yet. And in the meantime mamma, and papa too, sometimes had tea with the little girls and Randolph.

The fire was burning brightly and the table looked inviting when Mrs. Vane came downstairs. Alie had hurried down to see to it all; she knew what a difference a little care makes sometimes — how a crumpled-looking table-cloth or untidily placed dishes will add to low spirits when any one is not feeling as bright and cheerful as usual. There were still some of grandmamma's good things, which she had had packed in a hamper for the first start at the new rectory — home-made cakes and honey and fresh butter, the very sight of which made one hungry!

Rosalys glanced at her mother, and was pleased to see that the sweet face looked rather brighter and less anxious as she stood for a moment at the fire warming her hands.

'There is one comfort in this house, inconvenient though it is in many ways,' said Mrs. Vane, 'the chimneys don't smoke. And close to the sea as it is, one could scarcely have wondered if they had done so. If only it really does your father as much good as the doctors said, I am sure I shall get to like it.'

'Yes indeed,' Alie agreed. 'Mamma dear, won't you sit down and let me pour out your tea?'

'The wind is really rising,' said Mrs. Vane. 'I wish they would come in — papa and Rough. It would be such a pity if he caught cold,' she added with a little sigh.

Something in the tone and the sigh caught Biddy's attention. She was sitting at the table more silent than usual, very much absorbed, in fact, with her own grievances. What did mamma mean?

'Is papa ill?' she asked abruptly.

Alie glanced at her, frowning slightly. Her mother turned quickly.

'What a strange question to ask, Bride,' she said; 'it is just like you — you cannot but know that papa is not at all strong.'

Biddy looked puzzled. 'Strong' to her meant vaguely being able to lift heavy weights, or things of that kind.

'I didn't know he was *ill*,' she replied. 'I didn't know big people were ill except for going to die, like our 'nother grandmamma. Papa's had the measles and chicken-pox when he was little, hasn't he? I thought it was only children that could be ill to get better like that.'

Mrs. Vane glanced at Rosalys in a sort of despair. But before Alie could say anything to smooth matters, her mother called Bridget from her seat and made her stand before her.

'Bridget,' she said, 'I don't know what to say to you. Have you no heart or feeling at all? How *can* you say such things. I do not believe in your not understanding; you can understand when you choose, and you are nearly eight years old. You must know how miserably anxious I have been and still am about your father; you *must* know it is for his health we have come to this strange, dreary place, away from every one we care for, and you can talk in that cold-hearted, cold-blooded way about dying and not getting better and — and — ' Mrs. Vane's voice trembled and quivered. She seemed almost as if she were going to cry. Alie came and stood beside her, gently putting her arm round her mother and looking daggers at Bride. Mamma was nervous and over-tired, she knew; she had had so much to go through lately. How could Biddy be so naughty and unfeeling? And yet, as the words passed through her mind, Rosalys hesitated. Biddy was not really unfeeling — it was not the word for her. It was more as if she would not take the trouble to feel or to understand anything that was not her own special concern; there was a queer kind of laziness about her, which led to selfishness. It was as if her mind and heart were asleep sometimes.

But she could feel. Her face was all puckered up now; there was no temper or sullenness about it, but real pale-faced distress.

'Mamma,' she said brokenly, 'I didn't, oh, truly, I didn't mean it that way. I know papa isn't old enough to die; but I thought he was too big to be ill like that.'

'Biddy,' said Alie sternly, 'you are talking nonsense again. You know big people are ill often, and sometimes they get better and sometimes they die. Don't you remember Mrs. Hay — Meta Hay's mamma? She was ill and — '

'Yes, I quite forgot,' exclaimed Biddy eagerly; 'I didn't think. Yes, Meta's mamma was very ill, and she died. I wish I'd remembered; and she wasn't at all old like Grandmamma Vane.'

She spoke almost cheerfully. Again Mrs. Vane glanced at her elder daughter.

'It's no use,' she was beginning, but Alie interrupted. How she wished the unfortunate Mrs. Hay had not been the first instance to occur to her!

'*Children* get ill and die too sometimes,' Alie went on, 'and big people very often get better. There was Captain Leonard next door to us at home — '

'And — I know — the boy-that-brought-the-potatoes' papa,' cried Biddy. 'I *am* so glad I thought of him. I was in the kitchen one morning fetching sand for Tweetums's cage and he came in, and cook asked how was his papa, and he said, "Finely better, I thank ye, mum." I think cook said he was a *Hirish* boy,' Bridget hurried on in her excitement — and when she was excited I am afraid her 'h's' were apt to suffer — Mrs. Vane gasped! 'I am *so* glad I thought of him. Papa will get better like the potato boy's father. I'll say it in my prayers. Dear mamma, I won't forget. And I *will* try to be good and not tear my frocks nor speak without thinking.'

The tears were coming now, but Biddy knew mamma did not like her to begin to cry, and truly it was no wonder, for once she began it was by no means easy to say when she would leave off! She choked them down as well as she could. And the little face, hot and flushed now, was timidly raised to her mother's for a kiss of forgiveness.

It was not refused, but a sigh accompanied it, which went to the child's heart. But there was no time for more, as at that moment the hall door was heard to open and Mr. Vane's and Rough's voices sounded outside.

Quite subdued, desperately penitent, Bridget went back to her place. Her head was full as well as her heart. She had so many things to think over that she felt as if she could not eat. First and foremost was the strange newly awakened anxiety about her father. She looked at him as he came in as she had never looked at him before, almost expecting to see some great and appalling change in his appearance. But no — he seemed much as usual — his face was indeed reddened a little by his brisk walk in the chill air, and his voice was as cheery as ever. Biddy gave a loud, most audible sigh of relief. Mr. Vane started and interrupted himself in the middle of a lively account of the adventures he and Randolph had met with in their walk.

'My dear Biddy,' he said. 'What *can* you have to sigh about in that appalling way?'

Bridget opened her mouth as if to speak, but Rosalys, trembling as to what she might not be going to say, interrupted.

'Please, papa, don't ask her just now,' she said; 'do go on telling us about what sort of a place Seacove is,' and she added in a whisper, as she gave a little private tug to his sleeve, 'Biddy's been rather — tiresome, and if she begins to cry — '

CHAPTER IV

BIDDY HAS SOME NEW THOUGHTS

'O, children take long to grow.'
—Jean Ingelow.

Mr. Vane nodded in token of comprehending Alie's hint.

'You must walk to Seacove to-morrow and see it for yourselves,' he said.

'That is to say if it is fine,' said Mrs. Vane. 'Doesn't it look stormy tonight?'

'The wind is getting up, but that one must expect at this time of the year, and a good blow now and then won't hurt the girls. I feel ever so much the better for the touch of it we had this afternoon. I'm certain it is a very healthy place.'

Mrs. Vane smiled a little.

'I have noticed that that is generally said of places that have nothing else to recommend them. But no,' she went on, 'I must not begin by finding fault. If it proves to us a health-giving place I certainly shall like it, whatever else it is or is not. Did you go into the church this afternoon?'

'Just for a moment. Rough wanted to glance at it,' Mr. Vane replied, his tone sounding rather less cheerful.

'It looked very dingy and dismal,' Randolph said. 'It's all high pews and high-up windows, you know, mamma. Papa says it must have been built at the very ugliest time for churches, before they began to improve at all.'

'And there is nothing to be done to it,' said Mr. Vane. 'Even if we could attempt it and had the money, there would be endless difficulties in the way of prejudice and old associations to overcome.'

'And it is not as if we were really settled here,' said the children's mother. 'You must not take the church to heart, Bernard; you could scarcely expect anything better in a place like this.'

'No — it will be slow work to bring about any improvement in outlying places of this kind certainly,' Mr. Vane agreed. Then he brightened up a little. 'There is a very good organ, and I met the organist. He seems very hearty and eager.'

'That's a good thing. How did you come across him?' asked Mrs. Vane.

'We went to the stationer's to order the newspapers. I might of course have had them straight from town, but I think it is right to get what one can in the place, and it helps me to get to know the people a little. The organist — Redding is his name — was in the shop; I fancy he's a bit of a gossip, for he looked rather guilty when we went in, just as if they had been talking about us, and then he introduced himself. He's coming up to have a talk with me to-morrow.'

'It is quite a nice shop,' said Randolph. 'I expect it has some of the College custom. I saw some books with the College crest on lying about. You can get painting things there, Alie,' he added.

Rosalys looked interested, and Biddy's face grew some degrees less long.

'Is there a toy-shop?' she asked.

'There's better than a toy-shop — a wonderful sort of place they call a bazaar,' Rough replied. 'You may walk all round and look at the things without having to buy, and there's one part where all the toys are only a penny.'

Biddy clasped her hands in ecstasy.

'Oh, mamma,' she said, '*may* we go and see it to-morrow? Oh, I'm sure Seacove is ever so much nicer than London!'

Mr. Vane smiled.

'How many pennies have you got to spend, Biddy?' he said.

Biddy's face sobered again, and the corners of her mouth went down.

'I've got two,' she said in a very meek voice, 'and there would have been another to-morrow, that's Saturday, if — I — hadn't — '

'What?' asked Mr. Vane.

'Tore my frock,' said Biddy very slowly.

'*Torn*, if you please,' said her father. 'Well, suppose mamma lets you off as it's the first Saturday at Seacove, that will be threepence, and suppose I give you three pennies more, that will be sixpence — with sixpence you could make important purchases at the penny counter, could she not, Rough?'

'Certainly, I should say,' Randolph replied.

Bridget's face crimsoned with pleasure. She got up from her seat and ran round to the arm-chair by the fire where Mr. Vane was quietly sipping his tea, and at the imminent risk of throwing it all over him, flung her arms round his neck.

'Oh, thank you, papa, *dear* papa,' she said, 'dear, dear papa, and I do *so* hope you'll be like the boy-that-brought-the-potatoes' papa, and I'm going always to be good now, always.'

Poor Mr. Vane disengaged himself and his tea-cup with some difficulty from his little daughter's embraces. To his surprise, when he could manage to see her face, there were tears in her eyes. He was touched but at the same time rather apprehensive; it was ticklish work when Biddy's floodgates were opened.

'My poor little woman,' he said; 'yes, it's quite right to make good resolutions. But, remember, Rome wasn't built in a day, Bride; you'll have to keep up your courage and go on trying. But what's all that about boys and potatoes?'

Biddy grew red; she felt by instinct that she must not tell over all the conversation; mamma would be vexed.

'I only meant — ' and she hesitated.

'Biddy knew a little greengrocer boy in London who was very fond of his father,' said Rosalys quickly.

'Never mind about that just now,' Mrs. Vane added. 'I have several things I want to ask you about your study. If you have finished your tea, will you come in there with me? The work-people about here are rather stupid, I'm afraid, Bernard. They don't the least understand about the book-shelves.'

'Don't worry yourself about it,' Mr. Vane replied. 'Things will get straight by degrees. I'm afraid you have much more trouble now that M'Creagh's gone.'

M'Creagh was Mrs. Vane's 'old maid,' as the children called her. She had been with her since Mrs. Vane's childhood, and had lately given up her right to the title by getting married, to the great regret of everybody except, I *fear*, Biddy. For M'Creagh had 'managed' the little girl in a wonderful way; that is to say, she had kept her in order, and Biddy very much preferred being left to her own devices.

Mrs. Vane sat down on the low couch — one end of which was covered with piles of books, — they were in the study by this time.

'Yes,' she said, 'I miss M'Creagh, but my real trouble just now, Bernard, is Biddy. I am afraid I don't take the right way with her, somehow. She is so tiresomely heedless and provoking, and sometimes I really wonder if she has any heart.'

Mr. Vane looked up in surprise, in which there was a little touch of indignation, at this. Fresh from Bridget's loving hugs and the sight of the tears in her eyes, he could hardly be expected to agree with this opinion of her.

'My dear,' he said, 'I think you are not fair upon her. I really can't help saying so. The poor child is heedless and provoking to a degree, but she is very affectionate.'

Mrs. Vane did not seem annoyed; she was, on the contrary, rather glad of what Mr. Vane said.

'Yes, she seems so sometimes, and I hope it is only her childishness — but it is so impossible to make any lasting impression on her. And I don't see how things are to improve with her. Rosalys was a perfect little woman at her age. Bridget thinks of *nothing* — I have seen it so much since we came here and during the bustle of the removal from London. She lives like a complete baby — perhaps it is partly that Alie is so unusually thoughtful and helpful, a real right-hand to me, and Rough too for a boy is very sensible. So Biddy goes her own way, nothing is expected of her, and she certainly fulfils the expectation,' she wound up with a half smile.

Mr. Vane sat silent.

'She might be better with some companionship of her own age,' he said in a few minutes. 'The give-and-take of even childish companionship is a kind of training and discipline. As it is, she is almost like an only child. Now, if Alie were away for a while, Bridget would have to try to take her place.'

'I could not do without Alie, not just now certainly,' said Mrs. Vane decidedly. 'We must just hope that somehow time will improve Bridget.'

'And don't be too hard on her,' said her father. 'I feel sure she means well.'

'When she means anything,' replied Mrs. Vane; 'but she seldom thinks enough for that.'

'I don't know about that,' said Mr. Vane doubtfully, 'still — '

But then something in the arrangement of the book-shelves caught his eye, and no more was said of Biddy for the time.

Papa did not forget. Bridget got her fourpence the next day, a penny from mamma and threepence from papa. And all troubles were thrown to the winds, torn frocks and everything disagreeable forgotten, when she set off with Rosalys and Randolph, under their maid's charge, for a visit to Seacove, the wonderful bazaar being the real object of the walk.

Only a very slight misgiving came over her as papa stooped to kiss her in the doorway; they met him on their way out.

'Be a sensible little woman today, my Biddy,' he said, 'and don't get into any scrapes to worry your mamma.'

The child looked up into his face. Was it the yellowish morning light from over the sea — for it was clear and bright though cold — that made papa's face so pale? And yesterday he had looked so nice and rosy — Biddy felt rather strange; for the first time in her little life there came over her a faint, very faint shadow of *the* shadow which, as we grow older, we learn cannot be avoided; the wings of the solemn angel seemed for an instant to brush her softly. Biddy trembled without understanding why.

'Papa, dear papa,' she said, but somehow no other words would come.

He kissed her again, and he smiled. It seemed to brighten up his face. Bridget gave a sigh of relief: the potato boy's papa had got well, and very likely he too looked pale sometimes. Still that strange breath of feeling had left some result.

'Alie,' she said, as she trotted down the garden path beside her sister, the sixpence tightly clasped in her hand, 'is there anything I could get for a present for two of my pennies? I want to get some of the toys for myself with papa's three pennies, and I want to get a thimble with one, 'cos I've lost mine, and my workbox is messy-looking.'

'You can't get a proper one for a penny, not a silver one, and mamma says imitation ones are bad to wear,' said Rosalys. 'I've got my first thimble that's too small now — it's real silver. I'll give it you, and that'll leave you threepence for your present. But who's it for?'

'Three pennies won't do,' said Biddy. 'It must be two pennies, 'cos it's for papa, and he gave me three pennies, and it would just be like giving it him back again.'

Rosalys and Randolph glanced at each other. They could scarcely believe it was thoughtless Biddy speaking.

'Yes, I quite understand,' said Alie. 'Let's see — what could you get for papa? Can't you help us, Rough?'

Rough considered deeply.

'A purse — no, that would be too dear — or an inkstand?' he said.

'I'm sure an inkstand would be far dearer,' said Alie sharply. 'You're no good, Rough. I daresay we'll see something there, Biddy dear. I'll not forget.'

Bride felt very pleased. She was in high favour with Rosalys, she could see. She began jumping up and down the little grass-covered sandy hillocks that bordered the road, scarcely more than a cart-track, across the common between the Rectory and the little town.

'There's a shorter way if we turn, a little farther on,' said Rough. 'We can either get on to the road above the shore — it's a proper road — or cut across a very sandy place, much sandier than the common.'

'No,' said Alie, 'I'd rather go along the road even if it's farther. Walking on sand is so tiresome, and spoils one's boots so. Biddy, I think you'd better walk quietly: remember what papa said, and you know you are rather unlucky.'

It was pleasant walking along the firm, hard road, and the fresh air was exhilarating — the sunshine, thin and wintry though it was, gilded palely the little shallow lakes and pools left by the outgoing tide along the shore, for it was almost low water now. Even the bare stretches of sand did not look ugly, as they sometimes do — a touch of sunshine makes all the difference! And the even stony path — a sort of natural breakwater running out towards the lighthouse — here and there caught a gleam or two from the sky.

'It looks quite different to last night,' said Alie. 'That's one thing I like the seaside for; it's always changing.'

'And the wind's gone down with the tide,' said Randolph, 'though it did blow last night. There'll be rough weather before long, everybody says.'

'I *would* so like to be in the lighthouse if there was a storm,' said Biddy. 'That isn't naughty to wish, Alie, for the lighthouse is to keep away shipwrecks. And if there just *was* one, you know, it *would* be nice to be there to help the poor wet people, and carry them in to the fire, and rub them dry with hot blankets, like in that story, you know.'

'A lot you'd be able to carry,' said Rough contemptuously. 'Why, you're so fat and roundabout, and your legs are so short you can scarcely carry yourself.'

'Rough,' began Rosalys warningly. And

'*Alie,*' began Bridget at the same moment in her whining tone, 'do listen to him.'

But a peremptory 'Hush' from Randolph checked her. Both the girls looked up. A short, rather stout, pleasant-faced man was at that moment overtaking them.

'Good-morning, sir,' he said as he passed, and 'Good-morning, Mr. Redding,' returned Rough courteously, as the other lifted his hat. Rough had very nice manners.

'That is Redding, the organist,' said Rough. 'He's something else as well — a tailor or a draper — '

'"A butcher, a baker, or candlestick-maker,"' interrupted Rosalys laughingly. She did not mean to make fun of good Mr. Redding, but she wanted to make the others laugh too, to restore their good humour.

'Well, something, any way,' Randolph went on. 'Papa says he's an awfully good sort of man; he gives all his spare time to the organ for nothing.'

'That's very nice,' said Alie approvingly.

They were near the actual town of Seacove by this time — town or village, it was difficult to say which, though the rows of tall masts a little way off in the docks and the paved streets hardly seemed to suit the idea of a village. And a few minutes more brought them to what was ambitiously called the 'Parade,' where stood the long low bazaar, with a large placard at the door announcing that 'entrance' was 'free.'

In summer the bazaar blossomed out into twice its winter size, thanks to a tentlike canvas front; at present it was a building of not very imposing appearance. But it was long in proportion to its width, and one or two gas-jets lighted up the innermost end, even in the daytime. This gave it a rather mysterious air, and added much to Biddy's admiration.

'It's a *lovely* place,' she whispered to the others in an almost awestruck tone. Rough felt much gratified; he considered the bazaar his own 'find.' He set to work very graciously to do the honours of it, and led the way slowly between the two sloping-upwards counters or tables at each side, on which were arranged the more important and expensive wares — china vases, glass, English and foreign, some of it really quaint and uncommon, such as was not, in those days at least, to be often met with in regular shops, workboxes and desks of various kinds; papier-mâché writing-books, a few clocks; jewelry, a little real, a great deal imitation, in glass-lidded cases; and so on. And down the centre stood groups of walking-sticks, camp-stools, croquet-sets, and such like.

'Usefuller' things, as Biddy afterwards told her mother, were not wanting either. Hair-brushes and combs, metal teapots, and lots of gaily painted trays were among them. And some very magnificent dolls gazed down with their bright unblinking eyes at the whole from a high position, where they and the larger, more costly toys were placed.

It was all very imposing, very breath-taking-away, and Biddy's eyes were very eager and her mouth wide open as she trotted after Alie. For London shops were not as magnificent forty years ago as they are now; and, besides it was not often that the little Vanes had paid a visit to Cremer's or the arcades, which are children's delight. And then it was here so delightfully uncrowded and quiet. The shopwoman, knowing who they were, felt not a little honoured by their prompt visit, and beyond a civil 'Good-morning, young ladies,' left them free to stare about and admire as they chose.

But they did not linger long before the objects which they knew to be quite beyond their reach. It was the penny counter for which they were really bound, and to which Rough piloted them with an air of great pride.

'There, now,' he said, waving his hand like a show-man; 'what do you say to that, girls? All these things — everything you can see as far as here — for a penny!'

Biddy gasped; even Alie was impressed.

'They're really very nice, Biddy,' she said. 'And oh, look, what nice dolls' furniture! What a pity, Biddy, you don't care for dolls!'

CHAPTER V

CELESTINA

'Little china tea-things and delightful dinner-sets;
Trumpets, drums, and baby-horses; balls in coloured nets.'
—What the Toys do at Night.

Just as she said these words Rosalys became conscious that some one else was standing beside her. She looked round. A little girl, simply but neatly dressed, had come into the bazaar, and had made her way noiselessly up to where the Rectory children stood. She was a slight, delicate-looking child, taller than Bridget, though not seemingly much older. She had large, earnest, perhaps somewhat wistful, brown eyes, which made her face attractive and interesting when you looked at it closely, though at first sight it was too small and pale to catch one's attention. She stood there quietly and very grave, her eyes fixed on Alie Vane's lovely and sweet face, yet without the slightest shadow of forwardness or freedom in her gaze. An expression of great surprise, mingled with a little pity, flitted across her when she heard the elder girl's words — 'What a pity, Biddy, you don't care for dolls!' and it was with intense interest she listened to Bridget's reply.

'I would care for them, Alie, if I had any one to play at them with me. But you think you're too big — I think you've always thought yourself too big — and Rough's a boy. So how could I care for dolls all alone?'

Bride's voice had taken the peculiar little whine it always did when she was at all put out. It was comical and yet a little irritating; but just now neither Rosalys nor Randolph was inclined to be irritated. Alie only laughed.

'Well, I'm not forcing you to play with dolls, nor to buy them,' she said. 'Only these little tiny chairs are so funny.'

A voice behind her made her start. Yet it was a very soft, rather timid little voice.

'You can play much nicer with little dolls alone — a good many little dolls — than with one or two big ones,' it said.

Biddy turned round and stared at the small maiden. She did

not mean to be rude; she was only surprised and curious; but her rosy cheeks and round eyes looked much less sweet and gentle than Alie's pretty face and soft long-lashed blue eyes, which had always a rather appealing expression. Biddy opened her mouth but did not speak. The little stranger grew very red. Rosalys spoke to her gently.

'Yes,' she said, 'I should think little dolls would be much more amusing to play with alone. You could make them act things, and you could make houses for them. Biddy, wouldn't you like to furnish our old doll-house fresh?'

'I don't know,' said Biddy rather surlily. 'You'd call me a baby.'

'Indeed I wouldn't,' said Alie eagerly. 'It would be such a nice play for you. You might buy two or three of those sweet little chairs as a beginning.'

'They are particular nice,' put in the shopwoman. 'It isn't often they're made so small, not so cheap. And what were you wanting this morning, my dear?' she went on to the little newcomer.

'If you please, I want two of them — of the chairs,' the child replied, holding out two pennies. Her face was still rather red, but she glanced with admiration mingled with gratitude at Rosalys.

The shopwoman handed her the two little chairs, but she did not seem quite satisfied.

'Would you like to choose for yourself?' said the woman with a smile. She seemed used to the ways and manners of small customers — of this small customer especially, perhaps — and she made way for her as the little girl, well pleased, came close to the counter. Then for a minute or two the child stood absorbed, weighing the comparative merits of blue and pink cotton chair seats, and of dark and light coloured wood. At last, with a little sigh of mingled anxiety and satisfaction, she held out two to the woman.

'These, please,' she said; and, without waiting for her purchases to be wrapped up, she turned, and with a glance at the other children, a shadowy smile for half an instant wavering over her face, she quietly made her way out of the shop.

'Poor little girl,' said Rosalys. 'You quite frightened her when she spoke, Bridget. Why did you glare at her so?'

'I didn't glare at her; you're very unkind, Alie, to say so,' said Biddy, in her complaining tone.

'Oh, I say, Biddy, don't be so grumpy,' Randolph put in, 'and do fix what you're going to buy. There's something over here that papa would like, I know. A whistle, such a jolly strong one, and only two-pence. It would do for him to call me in by, and much less trouble than ringing that clumsy bell.'

Biddy went off to look at the whistle. It was a very neat one, in the shape of a dog's head, and she at once decided upon it, for she had great faith in Rough's opinion as to what papa would like. Then ensued another weighty consultation at the penny stall, where Alie had meantime bought a pair of tiny dolls, which she meant to dress in secret as a 'surprise' for her little sister — 'it would be so nice if she took to dressing dolls for herself,' she thought — and a yard measure for herself. Bridget's perplexities ended in the purchase of one of the neat little chairs and a small table and a tiny china dog.

'They'd be pretty as ornaments on my mantelpiece even if I never have a doll-house,' she said. 'And if I did have the doll-house done up, it *must* have a dog, to keep watch, you know, Alie.'

At the entrance of the bazaar they ran against Mr. Redding. He looked hot and hurried and was walking very fast, but at sight of them he stopped suddenly, and then, came up to Randolph.

'*Would* you excuse me, sir,' he began, 'if I were to ask you a great favour? I have just been at the Rectory to see Mr. Vane and I am hurrying off to Brewton by the next train, for unfortunately there is something wrong with one of the organ stops and I must get a man to come over at once. It would never do not to be able to use the organ properly the first Sunday Mr. Vane is here. I find it later than I thought, and I had undertaken to leave this note at Mr. Fairchild's in Pier Street for the rector. You will pass there on your way home, unless you particularly want to go by Sandy Common?'

'Oh no,' said Rough, 'we don't mind. Of course I'll leave it for you, Mr. Redding. Is there an answer?'

But Mr. Redding, having thrust the note into the boy's hands, was already some paces off. He called out some rather incoherent reply, of which 'thank you, thank you,' were the only intelligible words.

'What a fussy little man,' said Alie. 'But papa said he was proud of his organ, and it would be horrid at church without it. Which is Pier Street, Rough, do you know?'

'Not a bit of it — nor which is Mr. Fairchild's shop, or if it is a shop. He only said at Mr. Fairchild's,' replied Randolph. 'I suppose any one can tell us however; it's not like London.'

The 'Parade' at its farther end turned into the docks. The children walked on, tempted by the sight of the tall masts in front of them.

'Wouldn't I like to see over some of those ships,' said Rough. Just then a little group of sailors, looking little more than boys for the most part, in spite of their bronzed and sunburnt skin, passed them, chattering and whistling cheerily. They belonged to a vessel but newly arrived from some southern port. One could see how happy they were to be on English ground again — some of them maybe belonged to Seacove itself.

'Would you like to be a sailor, Rough?' said Alie.

Randolph hesitated.

'No, I don't think so, but I like seeing ships and hearing about voyages.'

'*I'd* like to be a sailor,' said Bridget suddenly. Rosalys and her brother could not help laughing.

'What a funny sailor you'd make,' they said. And indeed it was not easy to imagine her short, compact, roundabout figure climbing up masts and darting about with the monkey-like swiftness of a smart little middy.

'I don't think you'd like it for long, Miss Biddy,' said Jane, the young maid. 'I came once, in my last place, from Scotland by sea, and though I wasn't at all ill, it was dreadful rough work. I was glad to feel my feet on firm land again.'

'Was it very stormy?' asked all the children together. 'And how long were you in the ship? Oh, do tell us about it, Jane.'

Jane's value rose immensely on the spot. She was not a particularly lively girl generally, but this was quite a discovery.

'Was it a very big ship?' asked Bridget, 'or quite a teeny-weeny one, just big enough to hold all of us like?'

'You stupid little goose,' said Rough. 'You mean a boat — a *ship* is never as little as that.'

'Boats and ships is all the same,' Biddy persisted; 'and I heard papa say there was a Scotch boat to Seacove twice a week — there now, Rough.'

'Oh well — but that's only a way of speaking. Papa didn't mean a real boat — a little boat. Now, if we could go down those steps right among all the ships I'd soon show you the difference.'

'But we mustn't, Rough,' said Alie anxiously. 'Not without papa or somebody big — any way we must ask leave first.'

'Well, I suppose it would hardly do for you girls,' Rough replied. 'But of course papa would let *me* go. He and I walked all round the docks last night, and we should have gone to the end of the pier if — '

'Oh, that reminds me,' said Rosalys. 'Haven't we passed Pier Street? I believe that must be it opposite. Yes, I see it put up. Now we must find out Mr. Fairchild's. Can't you ask somebody, Rough?'

Randolph, though he would not have confessed it, was a little shy of accosting any of the few passers-by. Just because there were so few and the place was so quiet, the children felt themselves rather uncomfortably conspicuous, and they could not help noticing that here and there the inhabitants came rather unnecessarily to their doors to look at them as they passed. It was not done rudely, and indeed it was only natural that the arrival of a new rector and his family at Seacove should attract a good deal of attention, considering that old Dr. Bunton and his wife had been fixtures there for more years than Mr. Vane himself had been in the world.

'Oh yes,' said Rough in an off-hand way, 'I can ask any one. But we may as well walk on a little and look about us. If it is a shop we'll see the name.'

Just then there came out of a shop in front of them — a baker's, I think it was — a small figure which walked on slowly some paces before them.

'That's the little girl of the dolls' chairs,' exclaimed Bridget.

'Shall I run on and ask her? I don't mind.'

'You never do,' said Alie, and indeed Biddy was most comfortably untroubled with shyness.

'Yes, run on and see if she knows where it is.'

Off trotted Biddy, her precious purchases tightly clasped in her hands.

'Little girl,' she called, when she got close to the other child.

The little girl turned, and looked at Biddy full in the face with her grave earnest eyes without speaking. And for half a moment Bridget did feel something approaching to shyness, but it gave her a comfortable fellow-feeling to see that the small stranger was also still carrying the little chairs she had bought. They were not done up in paper like Biddy's — she had not waited for that, — but she had covered them loosely with a very clean, very diminutive pocket-handkerchief, and Bridget saw quite well what they were.

'Please,' Biddy went on, slightly breathless — it did not take much to put Biddy out of breath — 'please can you tell us where Mr. Fairchild's is in this street? Rough's got a letter for him, but we don't know if it's a shop or only a house.'

'Mr. Fairchild's,' repeated the little girl, 'he's my father; it's our shop. I'll show it you,' and a faint pink flush of excitement came into her pale face. These were the Rectory young ladies, she had been sure of it when she saw them in the bazaar. Fancy — wouldn't mother be surprised to see them coming in with her? And father, who had said she'd maybe never see them. Was that the French ma'amselle with them? — and Celestina glanced back at honest Jane Dodson, from 'grandmamma's' village, walking along in her usual rather depressed fashion — if so, French ma'amselles were very like English nurse-maids, thought her little observer.

'How funny!' said Biddy, quite interested. And Celestina began to like her better — she had been rather disappointed in Biddy at the bazaar. She was not pretty, and Celestina, though she scarcely knew it, was very much taken by beauty, and she had been rather, almost a little rude — at least Celestina knew that *she* would have been told she was rude had she behaved as Bridget had done. But now she seemed so bright and natural — 'She is quite a little girl,' thought Celestina; 'and perhaps if she's the youngest she's treated rather like a baby.' 'How *very* funny!' Biddy repeated. 'I must run back and tell Alie and Rough. And have you a doll-house, little girl, and will you show it me? I've bought a chair too and a table. Perhaps if I saw your doll-house and teeny-weeny dolls I'd get to like to play with them too. We have a — Oh, Alie,' as Alie, surprised at the length and apparent friendliness of the conversation proceeding between the two children, hastened up. 'Oh, Alie, *isn't* it funny? She's his little girl. The note's for her house.'

Rosalys turned her soft blue eyes full on Celestina.

'How like an angel she is!' thought Celestina.

'Who's?' said Alie. 'Do you mean Mr. Fairchild's? Why don't you explain properly, Biddy?'

'Yes, that's it,' said the stranger child. 'I'm Celestina Fairchild. I'll show you the shop.'

'Thank you,' said the elder girl. But Biddy would scarcely let her say the two words. Her eyes were very open, looking rounder than ever.

'*What* a funny name!' she exclaimed. Biddy's collection of adjectives did not seem to be a very large one. 'Do say it again; oh, please do.'

'Biddy, I think you are rather rude,' said Alie severely. 'You wouldn't like any one to say your name was funny.'

'I didn't mean — ' began Bridget as usual, but Celestina quietly interrupted.

'I don't mind; she's only a little girl. Don't be vexed with her,' she said to Alie with a sort of childish dignity that seemed to suit her. 'I think my name *is* funny; mother called it me 'cos — , but p'raps we'd better go on. I've been out a good while and mother might be wondering what I was doing, and then if the letter for father matters much — '

'Yes,' said Alie; 'you're quite right; we'd better be quick.'

So the little party set off again up the street. Biddy and Celestina — for now that Biddy's interest was awakened in the stranger child she had no idea of giving her up to the others — in front; Rosalys and her brother following; Jane Dodson, discreet and resigned, bringing up the rear.

They had not far to walk, but Bridget's tongue made the most of its opportunities.

'Have you got a doll-house, then?' she inquired of Celestina; and as the little girl shook her head rather dolefully in reply, 'What do you get furniture' (Biddy called it 'fenniture') 'for, then? Is it for ornaments?'

'No; I've got a room, though not a doll-house,' Celestina replied. 'It once was a kitchen, but I played with it too much when I was little, and the things got spoilt. So father did it up for me with new paper like a parlour — a best parlour, you know. Not a parlour like you use every day.'

'I don't know what a parlour is,' said Biddy; 'we haven't got one at the Rectory, and we hadn't one in London either. We've only got a schoolroom, and a dining-room, and a droind-room, and a study for papa, and — '

'I forgot,' said Celestina. 'I remember mother told me that they don't call them parlours in big houses. It's a drawing-room I mean; only the dolls have their dinner in it, because I haven't got a dining-room. They haven't any bedroom either; but I put them to bed in a very nice little basket, with a handkerchief and cotton-wool. It's very comfortable.'

'Yes?' said Bridget, greatly interested, 'and what more? Tell me, please. It sounds so nice.'

'Sometimes,' Celestina went on — 'sometimes I take them to the country — on the table, you know — and then I build them a house with books. It does very well if it's only a visit to the country, but it wouldn't do for a always house, 'cos it has to be cleared away for dinner.'

Biddy's mouth and eyes were wide open.

'We have dinner in the dining-room with papa and mamma,' she said; 'so we don't need to clear away off the schoolroom table except for tea. That's in London. I don't know where we're to have tea here, when Miss Millet comes back. Don't you have dinner with your papa and mamma — when they have luncheon, you know?'

In her turn Celestina stared.

'I don't know how you mean. We all have dinner in the

parlour,' she said, 'like — like everybody. But this is our shop,' she added, stopping and turning so as to face the others. 'If you please, miss,' she went on to Rosalys, 'this is father's shop. If you'll come in, he'll be there.'

Not a little surprised was Mr. Fairchild to see his daughter showing the way in to the three children, whom he rightly and at once guessed to be the new rector's family. Celestina looked quite composed; though so very quiet and silent a child, she was neither shy nor awkward. She was too little taken up with herself to have the foolish ideas which make so many children bashful and unready: it never entered her head that other people were either thinking of or looking at her. So she was free to notice what she could do and when she was wanted, and her simple kindly little heart was always pleased to render others a service, however small.

'Father,' she said in her soft voice; 'it is young Master Vane and the young ladies with a letter for you.'

Mr. Fairchild came forward, out from behind the counter. He made a little bow to Rosalys, who was the foremost of the group, and a little smile brightened his thin face as his eyes rested on hers. Every one was attracted by Alie, and her voice was particularly gentle as she spoke to Mr. Fairchild, for the first thought that darted through her mind was, 'How very ill he looks, poor man — much worse than papa.'

'It is a letter for you, Mr. Fairchild,' she said. 'Mr. Redding asked my brother to give it to you. It is from pa — from Mr. Vane.'

'But I don't know if there is any answer,' said Rough. 'Redding didn't say. Please see, will you?'

Rosalys and Randolph and Jane in the doorway stood waiting while he read. But Biddy's eyes were hard at work. She caught Celestina as she was disappearing through an inner door.

'Oh, please,' she said, 'don't go away. Won't you show me your dolls? And oh, please, what *is* that funny little window up there in the wall? I would so like to look through it.'

CHAPTER VI

THE WINDOW IN THE WALL

'Will you step into my parlour?'
—The Spider and the Fly.

Celestina hesitated. She was anxious to be friendly to Bridget, and she had a strong instinct of hospitality, but the little girl rather took away her breath. Just at that moment, luckily, the door between the shop and the parlour — a door in the corner behind the counter — opened, just a little, enough to admit Mrs. Fairchild, who came in quietly. She had heard voices in the shop, and thought she was probably needed there, though at this time of the morning, especially when Celestina was out, she had to be sometimes in the kitchen.

'Celestina,' she exclaimed, surprised and not quite sure if she should be pleased, 'what are you doing? You should have come in at once. I have been expecting you.'

Then her eyes fell on the three — or four — three and a half, one might say, to be very correct — strangers in the shop, for Jane was still wavering on the doorstep, one foot on the pavement outside and one inside.

'Won't you come in?' said Mrs. Fairchild to her civilly; 'it is a cold morning — and then I could shut the door.'

Jane moved inwards, though without speaking, and Rough darted forward and shut the door carefully.

'Thank you, sir,' said Mrs. Fairchild, with a little smile that lighted up her whole face. She gave a half unconscious glance at her delicate-looking husband, which explained her anxiety. Bridget drew near her and looked up in her face. Somehow since Mrs. Fairchild had come in every one seemed more friendly and at ease.

'Are you Ce — Cel — the little-girl-in-the-bazaar's mamma?' asked Biddy.

Mrs. Fairchild smiled again.

'Yes,' she said, touching Celestina on the shoulder, 'I am *her* mother. Did you see her at the bazaar?'

'She was buying chairs, and that made me buy one too,' replied Biddy rather vaguely.

'The young ladies met me after that in the street and asked me the way here. I showed them. That was why I was in the shop,' explained Celestina, on whose brow a little wrinkle of uneasiness had remained till she could tell her mother the reason of her moment's lingering.

'I see,' said Mrs. Fairchild, who would indeed have found it difficult to believe that Celestina had been careless or disobedient; and at the words Celestina's face recovered its usual quiet, thoughtful, but peaceful expression.

Bridget pressed up a little closer to Mrs. Fairchild.

'You're not vexed with her then,' she said. 'She was quite good. I thought at first you were going to be rather a cross mamma.'

'*Bridget*,' said Rosalys, colouring, and in an awful tone. When Alie said 'Bridget' like that it meant a great deal.

'I didn't mean,' began Biddy as usual.

Celestina's mother turned to Rosalys.

'Please do not be vexed with her, miss,' she said, with again that winning smile. And the smile that stole over Alie's face in response made Mrs. Fairchild's gaze linger on the lovely child. 'No, my dear,' she went on, speaking now to Biddy, 'it was quite right of Celestina to show you the way; and I am glad you happened to meet her.'

During this time, which was really only a minute or so, for it takes much longer to relate a little scene of this kind than for it actually to pass, Mr. Fairchild had been busy with the contents of the envelope Randolph had given him. It contained, besides a note, a list of some books which Mr. Vane wished to have sent as soon as possible. After knitting his brows over this for some moments, the bookseller came forward.

'I find that Mr. Vane would like this order executed at once,' he said, addressing Randolph.

'I don't know, I'm sure,' said Rough; and indeed how was he to know, seeing that the letter had only been given over to his charge by Mr. Redding?

Mr. Fairchild looked perplexed.

'Oh,' he said, 'I thought that possibly you could have explained a little more fully' — then he considered again. 'I think perhaps I could send specimens of some of the hymn-books, and I can make out a list of the prices, etc., so that Mr. Vane would have no trouble in selecting what he requires. It will only take me a few minutes, and it would save time if — ' he hesitated. 'My errand-boy has gone some distance away this morning.'

'If you mean that it'll save trouble for me to carry the parcel, I don't mind,' said Rough in his boyish way.

Mr. Fairchild thanked him.

'I will see to it at once,' he said, and turning to his desk he began writing down the details of some books which he took down from the shelves behind.

The four children, Mrs. Fairchild, and Jane Dodson stood together in the middle of the shop; it was quite small, and with these six people it seemed crowded. There was only one chair, pushed up in a corner by the counter.

'It is draughty near the door, even when it is shut. Will you not come farther in, Miss Vane? or,' with a little hesitation, 'would you step into the parlour — there is a nice fire — and sit down for a few minutes?' said Mrs. Fairchild to Rosalys.

Rosalys began to thank her, but before she had time to do more than begin Bridget interrupted.

'Oh yes, Alie, please do,' she said eagerly. 'I do so want to see what a parlour's like. But, please,' she went on to Mrs. Fairchild, 'would you first tell me what that dear little peep-hole window up in the wall is for? I would so like to look through it.'

Alie's face grew red again; she really felt ashamed of Biddy.

'And it's worse,' she said to herself, 'to be so forward to people who are not quite the same as us, though I'm sure Mrs. Fairchild is as nice as any lady.'

And Mrs. Fairchild confirmed this feeling of Alie's by coming again to the rescue.

'Certainly, my dear,' she said, smiling. 'You shall look through the window from the other side. There's pretty sure to be a chair in front of it, if you are not tall enough. My little girl is very fond of looking through that funny window.'

She led the way through another door — a door facing the street entrance — into a very small passage, whence a narrow staircase ran up to the first floor. The children could scarcely see where they were, for the passage was dark, till Mrs. Fairchild opened another door leading into the parlour, and even then it was not very light, for the parlour window, as I think I said before, looked on to a little yard, and there were the walls of other houses round this yard.

It was a very neat, but to the children's eyes a rather dreary-looking little room.

Biddy turned to Celestina.

'I think I like droind-rooms better than parlours,' she said, returning to their conversation in the street, 'except for the sweet little window,' and in another instant she had mounted the chair and was peering through. 'Oh, it *is* nice,' she said. 'I can see Roughie' — for Rough, had considered it more manly to stay in the shop — 'and Mr. — your papa, Celestina. It's like a magic-lantern; no, I mean a peep-show. I wish we had one in our house. Alie, do look.'

Rosalys came forward, not so eager to take advantage of Biddy's obliging offer as to seize the chance of giving her a little private admonition.

'Biddy,' she whispered, 'I'm ashamed of you. I never knew you so free and rude before.'

Bridget descended dolefully from the chair.

'I'm very sorry,' she said; 'please, ma'am,' and she turned to Mrs. Fairchild, 'I didn't mean to be free and rude.'

The babyishness of her round fat face, and her brown eyes looking quite ready to cry, touched Mrs. Fairchild, though it is fair to add that she approved of Alie's checking the child. She would have been perfectly shocked if Celestina even when younger than Biddy had behaved to strangers as the little visitor was doing. Children were kept much more in the background forty years ago than now. On the whole I don't know that it was altogether a bad thing for them, though in some cases it was carried too far, much farther than you, dear children of today, would find at all pleasant, or than I should like to see.'

'No, my dear, I am sure you did not mean any harm,' said Mrs. Fairchild. 'We all have to learn, but it is very nice for you to have a kind elder sister to direct you.'

Biddy did not seem at that moment very keenly to appreciate this privilege.

'I'd rather have a littler sister,' she said; but as she caught sight of Celestina's astonished face, 'I don't mean for Alie to be away — Alie's very kind — but I'd like a littler one too. It's very dull playing alone. And oh, please,' as the word 'playing' recalled the bazaar and their purchases, 'mayn't I see her dolls' house?' and she pointed to Celestina.

Rosalys sighed. Bridget was incorrigible.

'It isn't a house,' said Celestina, 'it's only a room. May I get it, mother? I do so want to see if the new chairs will do,' she went on, for the first time disengaging the toys from her handkerchief. 'The others are so big that when the dolls sit on them their legs go all over the top of the table instead of underneath.'

'I know,' said Alie, 'that's how mine used to do when I was a little girl and played with our doll-house. But mamma got some for me from Germany all the proper size, on purpose. The doll-house was really very pretty then.'

Celestina looked up with eager eyes.

'Oh, I would like to see it,' she said. 'It must be beautiful.'

'No' said Rosalys, 'it isn't now. Some of the furniture's broken, and nearly all the chair-seats need new covers. But it might be made very nice with a little trouble, only you see Bridget has never cared to play with it.'

Biddy had drawn near and was standing listening.

'I daresay I would care if I had anybody to play with me,' she said. 'You know you're too big, Alie. I wish Celestina could come and play with me. Won't you let her, if mamma says she may?' she went on, turning to Mrs. Fairchild.

Celestina's eyes sparkled, but her mother looked rather grave.

'My dear young lady,' she said to Biddy, 'you are rather too young to plan things of that kind till you have talked about them to your mamma. Besides Celestina almost never goes anywhere.'

'I went to tea at Miss Bankes's once,' said Celestina. 'That's where I used to go to school, but I didn't like it much — they played such noisy games and they were all so smart. And once I went to Nelly Tasker's, and that was nice, but they've left Seacove a long time ago.'

Mrs. Fairchild looked at Celestina in some surprise. It was seldom the little girl was so communicative, especially to strangers. But then, as she said to her husband afterwards —

'Miss Vane is a very sweet girl, and the little one chatters as if she'd known you for years. They certainly have a very friendly way with them: I couldn't exactly wonder at Celestina.'

'I'll ask mamma. You'll see if I don't,' said Biddy, nodding her head with determination. 'And please, Celestina, do let me see your doll-room, if that's what you call it?'

'May I fetch it, mother?' asked the child. But at that moment Randolph put his head in at the door.

'We must be going,' he said. 'Come along, girls. I've got the parcel. Thank you,' he added to Mrs. Fairchild, 'and good-morning.'

Alie and Biddy turned to follow him. But first they shook hands with Celestina and her mother.

'I'm so sorry,' said Biddy, 'not to see the dolls' room. Wouldn't Rough wait a minute, Alie?'

'No,' the elder sister replied. 'We've been out a good while and there's no reason for waiting now the parcel's ready.'

'Well I'll come again. You'll let me, won't you?' said Bride, and not content with shaking hands, she held up her round rosy mouth for a kiss.

'Bless you, love,' kind Mrs. Fairchild could not resist saying, as she stooped to her.

'She is a very nice mamma, isn't she, Alie?' said Biddy with satisfaction, when they found themselves out in the street again.

'Yes,' said Rosalys. But she spoke rather absently. She was wondering what made Bridget so nice sometimes, and sometimes so very tiresome and heedless.

'I wonder if it would have been better for her if she was more like that little Celestina,' she thought. 'I'm sure they're very strict with her, and yet I'm sure she's very fond of her mother and very obedient. But it must be rather a dull life for a little girl, only she seems so womanly; as if she really felt she was useful.'

It was almost dinner-time — their dinner-time, that is to say — when the children reached the Rectory, and there was something of a scramble to get hands washed, hair smoothed, and thick boots changed so as to be in time and not keep papa and mamma waiting. Randolph came into the dining-room, carrying the parcel of books.

'Papa,' he said, 'these are the books you told Redding to order for you — at least there are some of them, and if they are right, or if you'll mark down which of them are not right, Fairchild the bookseller will order what you want at once.'

'I'll look at them immediately after luncheon,' Mr. Vane replied. 'But how did they come into your hands, my boy? Has Redding been here again?'

'No,' Rough explained, 'we met him,' and then he went on to tell the history of the morning.

'And she 'avited us — the little-girl-in-the-bazaar's mother, I mean,' Biddy hastened to add, 'to step into the parlour. I never saw a parlour before; it's not as nice as a droind-room, except for the dear little window up in the wall. Couldn't we have a little window like that in our schoolroom, mamma? And I'm to go another day to see the room; it's not a proper doll-house, she says; only a room, and I said I was sure I might ask her to come here, but she said I must ask my mamma first. I thought at first she was going to be rather a cross sort of a mamma, but I don't think she is — do you, Alie?'

Biddy ran off this long story so fast that Mrs. Vane could only stare at her in amazement.

'My dear Biddy!' she said at last. 'Alie, you were there? You don't mean to say that you let Bride run into the toy-shop people's house and make friends with their children, and — and — ' Mrs. Vane stopped short, at a loss for words.

Mr. Vane looked up.

'My dear child,' he said too, to Bridget, 'you must be careful. And here — where everybody is sure to know who you are, and when you should set a good example of nice manners — you must not behave in this wild sort of way.'

'I didn't mean,' began Biddy plaintively.

But this time she was not chidden for her doleful tone — both Alie and Rough came to the rescue.

'Please, mamma, oh please, papa, you don't understand,' began Rosalys.

'It wasn't the bazaar people at all,' said Rough, chiming in; 'it was all right. Only, Biddy, you are really too stupid, the muddley way you tell things — '

'Yes,' agreed Alie, with natural vexation, 'you needn't make it seem as if we had all gone out of our minds, really.'

'I didn't mean,' started Biddy again, and still more lugubriously.

'Stop, Bride,' said Mr. Vane authoritatively, laying down his knife and fork as he spoke. 'Now, Rosalys, tell the whole story properly.'

Alie did so, and as Randolph had already explained about meeting Mr. Redding, it was not long before his father and mother understood the real facts clearly.

'We couldn't have refused to go into the parlour when Mrs. Fairchild asked us like that — could we, mamma?' Rosalys wound up.

'And she asked us to step in so nicely. And there were no chairs in the shop, 'cept only one. And I did so want to see a parlour,' added Biddy, reviving under Alie's support.

'No, you did quite right,' said Mrs. Vane to the elder ones. 'But Biddy must not begin making friends with every child she comes across and inviting them to come here. You are not a baby now; you should have more sense.'

The tears collected in Bridget's eyes; they were very obedient to her summons, it must be allowed. Rosalys felt sorry for her.

'Mamma,' she said, 'of course Biddy shouldn't invite anybody without your leave first, but still this little Celestina isn't *at all* a common child. She's so neat and quiet, and she speaks so nicely. And her mother is *nearly* as pretty as you, not quite of course.'

'She's awfully jolly,' put in Rough.

Mrs. Vane smiled.

'What an uncommon name,' she said. '"Célestine," did you say? It is French.'

'No, mamma, not "Célestine,"' said Alie, '"Celestina." I suppose it's the English of the other.'

'I never heard it in English before,' said Mrs. Vane, 'though I once had a dear old friend in France called "Célestine" — you remember Madame d'Ermont, Bernard? I've not heard from her for ever so long.'

'Celestina was going to tell us about her name, but something interrupted her and then she forgot,' said Alie. 'Perhaps they've got some French relations, mamma.'

'It isn't likely,' her mother replied. 'But some day when I am in the village, or town — should we call it "town," Bernard?'

'It is a seaport, so it must be a town, I suppose,' said Mr. Vane.

'I should like to see the little girl and her mother,' Mrs. Vane continued.

'And oh, mamma,' cried Biddy, jumping up and down in her chair as her spirits rose again, 'when you do, *mayn't* I go with you, and then Celestina would show me her dolls' room?'

'We shall see, my dear,' her mother replied.

Biddy was not at all fond of the reply, 'We shall see.' 'It's only a perlite way of saying "no,"' she once said, but she dared not tease her mother any more.

'Nobody cares about what I like,' she said to herself disconsolately.

Perhaps she would not have thought so if she had heard what her mother and Rosalys were talking about later that afternoon.

CHAPTER VII
ON THE SEASHORE

'The sands of the sea stretch far and fine,
The rocks start out of them sharp and slim.'
—*A Legend of the Sea.*

'Oh dear,' exclaimed Mrs. Vane one morning at breakfast two or three days after the children's walk in to Seacove. Everybody looked up — the two girls and Rough were at table with their father and mother. Mrs. Vane had just opened and begun to read a letter. What could be the matter?

'It is from Miss Millet,' she said; 'her sister's children have got scarlet fever, and she has got a bad sore throat herself from nursing them. They had no idea what it was at first,' she went on reading from the letter; 'but of course she cannot come back to us for ever so long on account of the infection.'

'Poor Miss Millet,' said Rosalys.

'*I* don't mind,' said Biddy; 'I like having holidays.'

Alie, who was sitting next her, gave her a little touch.

'Hush, Biddy,' she said, 'that's just one of the things you say that sound *so* unkind.'

She spoke in a whisper, and fortunately for Bridget her father and mother were too much taken up with the letter to notice what she had said.

'I didn't mean,' Biddy was beginning as usual, but Mrs. Vane was speaking to Alie by this time, and no one listened to Biddy.

'I must write to Miss Millet at once,' their mother said, 'though I shall ask her not to write often till the infection is gone — she says this letter is disinfected. And, Alie, you had better put in a little word, and Biddy too, if she likes. It would be kind.'

'Yes, mamma,' said Alie at once, but Bridget did not answer.

It was not usual for Mrs. Vane to discuss plans and arrangements for the children before them, but this morning her mind was so full of the unexpected turn of affairs that she could not help talking about them.

'It will be a question of several weeks — even months, I fear,' she said to Mr. Vane; 'there are such a lot of those children, and Miss Millet is sure to wish to nurse them all. We must think over what to do.'

'Perhaps you and I can manage the girls between us,' said Mr. Vane.

'Alie perhaps,' began Mrs. Vane doubtfully.

'Yes,' said Bridget suddenly, to every one's astonishment, 'if it was only Alie. But it would never do for me. I'd be too much for you and papa, mamma.'

She spoke quite gravely, but the others had hard work not to laugh.

'How do you mean, Biddy?' asked her father.

'I'm very tiresome to teach; often I'm very cross indeed,' replied the child complacently.

'But you *need* not be; you can help being so if you try,' said Mr. Vane.

'Well, I don't like trying, I suppose it's that,' she answered.

For the moment her father thought it wiser to say no more.

Mr. Redding happened to call that morning, and at luncheon Mrs. Vane told Alie and Bride that she was going to Seacove, and they might go with her.

Alie's eyes sparkled.

'Are you going to — ' she began, and her mother seemed to understand her without any more words.

'Yes,' she said, 'I have got all the measures.'

'And oh, mamma,' asked Biddy, too full of her own ideas to notice these mysterious sayings, '*will* you go to Pier Street and let us show you where Celestina lives. And if you *could* think of something you wanted to buy, just any little thing, a pencil or some envelopes or anything — they've got *everything* — we might go into the shop, and I *daresay* if the nice mamma saw you, she'd ask you to step into the parlour too.'

'We shall see,' mamma replied.

But 'We shall see' was this time accompanied by a little smile, which made Bridget think that the 'We shall see' was perhaps a way of saying 'Yes.'

Mamma had several messages to do at Seacove, and though

Biddy was in a great hurry to get to Pier Street, she was rather interested in the other shops also. At the draper's, Mrs. Vane made some small purchases, as to which Alie showed great concern. One was of pretty pink glazed calico and of some other shiny stuff called 'chintz' — white, with tiny lines of different colours; she also bought some red cotton velvet and neat-looking white spotted muslin, and several yards of very narrow lace of a very small and dainty pattern, and other things, all of which interested Alie very much indeed, though after a while Biddy got tired of looking on, and went and stood at the doorway of the shop.

'I am sorry to give you the trouble of taking down so many things when I only want such a short length of each,' said Mrs. Vane civilly to the shopman — or shopwoman, I think it was. 'But the fact is I am buying all these odds and ends for my little girl's' — and here she glanced round to make sure that Bridget was out of hearing — 'for my little girl's doll-house, which needs doing up;' by which information Mrs. Cutter, the draper's wife, was much edified, repeating it to her special cronies at Seacove, together with her opinion that the new rector's wife was a most pleasant-spoken lady.

One or two other shops Mrs. Vane and Rosalys went into; a paper-hanger's for one, or rather a painter's, where wall-papers were sold; and an iron-monger's, where she bought two or three different kinds of small nails, tin tacks, and neat little brass-headed nails. Bridget stayed at the door of both these shops: she thought them not at all interesting, and mamma and Alie did not press her to come in. The little girl was in a great fidget to get to Pier Street, and stood murmuring to herself that she didn't believe they'd *ever* come; Alie might make mamma be quick, she knew how she, Biddy, wanted to see Celestina and her dolls' room.

'But nobody cares about what *I* want,' she added to herself, with the discontented look on her face which so spoilt its round rosy pleasantness.

Just then out came Mrs. Vane and Alie. They both looked pleased and bright, and this made Biddy still crosser.

'Well, now,' said her mother consideringly, 'is that all, Alie? Yes — I think it is. I must call at the grocer's on the way home, but

I think we pass that way. No — I don't remember anything else.'

At this Bridget could no longer keep silent.

'Oh, mamma,' she exclaimed, 'and you said you'd come to Celestina's house. It's too bad.'

Mrs. Vane looked at her in surprise.

'I did not say so, Biddy; I said we should see. And we are going there now. You have no reason to be so impatient and to look so cross,' and she turned and walked on quickly.

'Biddy,' said Alie, 'you're too bad really. You spoil everything.'

Then she ran after her mother, and Bridget followed them at some little distance.

They went directly down the street which a little farther on ran into Pier Street, Biddy feeling more and more ashamed of herself. How she wished she had been less hasty, and not spoken so rudely and crossly to her mother. It did seem true, as Alie said, that she spoilt everything. But she did not appear as sorry as she felt; indeed, her face had a rather sulky look when at last she came up to the others, who were waiting for her at the door of the shop.

'I am going in to see Mrs. Fairchild,' said her mother. 'I have something to ask her. You may come in too, Biddy, and I will ask to see the little girl too.'

A naughty spirit came over Biddy, even though in her heart she was sorry.

'No,' she said. 'I don't want to see the little girl, and I don't want to come in,' and her face grew still more sullen.

'Very well,' said her mother, 'stay there then.'

But as she entered the shop with Alie she whispered to her, 'I really don't know what to do with Biddy. She has such a *very* bad temper, Alie. Just when I am doing everything I can for her too.'

'Only she doesn't know about it, you see, mamma,' Alie replied. 'Still she is very cross, I know.'

Mrs. Fairchild was herself in the shop as well as her husband. As soon as she caught sight of Rosalys she seemed to know who Mrs. Vane was, and came forward with her gentle smile.

'I hope you will excuse my troubling you, Mrs. Fairchild,' said the rector's wife, 'but Mr. Redding, whom I saw this morning, thought you would be the best person to apply to about a little difficulty I am in.'

She half glanced round as if to see that no one was in the way, and with quick understanding Celestina's mother turned towards the inner door.

'Will you please step into the parlour a moment?' she said. 'We should be less interrupted.'

Bridget, standing by the half-open shop door, heard the words. She felt almost inclined to run forward and beg leave to go in too. But she knew she must first ask pardon of her mother for her naughtiness, and the idea of doing so before Mrs. Fairchild was not pleasant.

'If Celestina would come out herself I could ask her to ask mamma to speak to me,' thought Bridget. But no Celestina appeared.

'They will be so comfortable in that nice warm parlour,' thought Biddy; 'and I daresay Celestina will be showing Alie all her dolls and things,' for she had not noticed that just as Mrs. Vane went into the parlour she had said a word to Rosalys, who had stayed behind.

So Biddy stood outside, very much put out indeed. The ten minutes during which she had to wait seemed to her like an hour; and when Celestina's mother came to the door to show her visitors out, it was not difficult for her to see that the little girl was not in at all a happy frame of mind.

'Good-morning, Miss Bridget,' said Mrs. Fairchild.

'Good-morning,' Biddy could not but reply.

She did not even wonder how Mrs. Fairchild knew her name; she was so taken up with her own thoughts. She would have been rather surprised had she known that it was about her, poor little neglected, uncared for girl as she chose to fancy herself, that the two mothers had been speaking those long ten minutes in the parlour — 'Mayn't I see Celestina at all?' Biddy went on. 'I think Alie's very — '

'Very what?' said her mother. 'Alie has been quietly waiting in the shop for me as I told her.'

Alie came forward as she spoke.

'And Celestina is not in this morning,' said Mrs. Fairchild.

'She had a headache, so I have sent her out a walk.'

Thus all Biddy's temper and jealousy had been thrown away. She felt rather foolish as she followed her mother and Rosalys down the street.

After stopping for a moment at the grocer's, Mrs. Vane turned to go home by the Parade, the same way by which the children had come to Seacove that Saturday. It was a fine bright afternoon, still early — a little breeze blew in from the sea — the tide was far out.

'Mayn't we go home by the shore, mamma?' Alie asked. 'It is nice firm walking nearly all the way.'

Mrs. Vane consented: they all turned down a sort of short cart-track, leading through the stony shingle to the smooth sands beyond. The sun was still some height above the horizon, but the cold frosty air gave it already the red evening look. Glancing upwards at it Biddy remembered the day she had watched it setting and the good resolutions she had then made. She almost felt as if the sun was looking at her and reminding her of them, and a feeling of shame, not proud but humble, crept over her. She went close up to her mother and slipped her hand through her arm.

'Mamma,' she said very gently, 'I'm sorry for being so cross.'

'I am glad to hear you say so, Bride,' said her mother. She spoke very gravely, and at first Bridget felt a little disappointed. But after a moment's — less than a moment's — hesitation, the fat little hand felt itself clasped and pressed with a kindly affection that, truth to tell, Biddy was scarcely accustomed to. For there is no denying that she was a very trying and tiresome little girl. And Mrs. Vane was quick and sensitive, and of late she had had much anxiety and strain, and she was not of a nature to take things calmly. Rosalys was of a much more even and cheery temperament: she 'took after' her father, as the country-people say. It was not without putting some slight force on herself that Biddy's mother pressed the little hand; and that she did so was in great part owing to a sudden remembrance of some words which Mrs. Fairchild had said during their few minutes' conversation, which, as I told you, had been principally about Bridget.

'Yes,' Celestina's mother had replied in answer to a remark of the rector's wife, 'I can see that she must be a child who needs careful management. Firmness of course — but also the greatest, the very greatest gentleness, so as never to crush or repress any deeper feeling whenever it comes.'

And the words had stayed in Biddy's mother's mind. Ah, children, *how* much we may do for good, and, alas, for bad, by our simplest words sometimes!

So in spite of still feeling irritated and sore against cross-grained Biddy, her mother crushed down her own vexation and met the child's better mind more than half-way.

A queer feeling came over the little girl; a sort of choke in her throat, which she had never felt before.

'If mamma was always like that *how* good I would be,' thought Biddy, as she walked on quietly, her hand still on her mother's arm.

Suddenly she withdrew it with a little cry, and ran on a few steps. Some way before them a small figure stood out dark against the sky, from time to time stooping as if picking up something. Bridget had excellent eyes when she chose to use them.

'It's Celestina, mamma,' she exclaimed, running back to her mother and Alie. 'Mayn't I go and speak to her? She's all alone. Come, Smuttie — it'll be a nice run for you. I may, mayn't I, mamma?'

'Very well,' said her mother, and almost before she said the words Biddy was off.

'She must be a nice little girl,' said Mrs. Vane; 'her mother seems such a sweet woman. But, Alie, did you ever see anything like Bride's changeableness?' and she gave a little sigh.

'But, mamma dear, she did say she was sorry very nicely this time — very *real*-ly,' said Rosalys.

'Yes, darling,' her mother agreed.

A minute or two brought them up to where the two children were standing talking together, greatly to Bridget's satisfaction, though Celestina looked very quiet and almost grave.

'How do you do, my dear?' said Mrs. Vane, shaking hands with her. 'I have just seen your mother; she said you were out a walk, but we did not know we should find you on the shore. Is it not rather lonely for you here by yourself?'

'I was looking for shells, ma'am,' Celestina replied. 'There's very pretty tiny ones just about here sometimes, though you have to look for them a good deal; they're so buried in the sand.'

'But she has found such beauties, and she takes them home for her dolls to use for dishes, and some of them for ornaments,' said Biddy. 'Do show mamma how *sweet* they are, Celestina. And oh, mamma, mayn't I stay a little with Celestina and look for them too?'

Mrs. Vane hesitated.

'I'm afraid not, Biddy,' she said. 'I must be going in — and Alie too. She must write to grandmamma today.'

'Oh, but mayn't *I* stay?' asked Biddy entreatingly. 'It's quite safe for me if it's safe for Celestina, and she says her mamma often lets her come out on the shore alone.'

Mrs. Vane looked round; the seashore was perfectly quiet except for one or two old fishermen mending their nets at some distance. One could have thought it miles away from the little port and the ships and the sailors. Then, too, the Rectory was a very short distance off, and indeed from its upper windows this sheltered stretch of sand could be clearly seen.

'Well, yes,' she said. 'You may stay for half an hour or so — not longer. And indeed by then it will be quite time for you too to be going home, will it not, my little girl?' she added to Celestina.

'Yes, ma'am. I must be home by half-past four, and it takes twenty minutes from here. I can go past the Rectory and see Miss — ' she hesitated over the name, 'Miss Biddy in at the gate, if you please,' said Celestina, in her womanly little way.

Mrs. Vane thanked her; then she and Rosalys walked on, and the two small damsels were left alone.

'Why must you be in by half-past four?' asked Biddy.

'It's getting dark by then,' said Celestina. 'Besides there's things to do. I get the tea ready very often. When mother's not very busy it waits for her till she can leave the shop, but today I know she's busy, 'cos father's got a great many letters to write. So I'll get the table all ready.'

Bridget gazed at her.

'Do you like doing it?' she asked. 'You're such a little girl, you see — not much bigger than me, and you play with dolls.'

'I like to be useful to mother,' said Celestina simply.

This was rather a new idea to Bridget, and she was sometimes very lazy about thinking over new ideas.

'Alie's useful to mamma, I suppose,' she said, 'but then she's the eldest. And you're the only one — that's why, I daresay. Is it nice to be the only one?'

'Sometimes it's very alone,' said Celestina, 'some days when mother's very busy and I scarcely see her, and I've nobody to show the dolls to.'

'I know,' said Biddy. 'I'm rather alone too, for Alie's so big, you see. Oh, Celestina, do look, isn't this a beauty? Look, it's all pinky inside. Now I've got six and this beauty. I think that'll do for today. I'm tired of looking.'

'Sometimes I look for ever so long — a whole hour,' said Celestina, rather taken aback by Biddy's fitfulness. 'But perhaps we'd better run about a little to keep warm. It isn't like as if it was summer.'

'I'm not cold and I don't like running,' said Biddy. 'Let's just walk, Celestina, and you tell me things. Oh, look at the sun — he's getting redder and redder — and look at the lighthouse, it's shining red too. Is it a fire burning inside, do you think, Celestina?'

'No, it's the sun's redness shining on the glass. The top room is all windows — I've been there once,' she said. 'It's a good way to walk though it looks so near, and there's some water too between. Father took us once in a boat, mother and me, when the tide was in, and we had dinner there; we took it with us, and there was a nice old man father knew. And when the tide went out we came over a bit of water till we got to the stones, in the boat, and then the boatman took it back, and we walked home right along the stones — you see where I mean?'

She pointed to the rocky ridge which I told you ran out from the shore to the lighthouse. Bridget listened with the greatest interest.

'How nice,' she said. 'Couldn't you have walked the whole way? I'm sure there isn't any water between now — *I* can't see it. It must have gone away.'

'Oh no, it hasn't,' said Celestina. 'It's always there: it couldn't go away. You couldn't ever get to the lighthouse without a boat; once one of the men had to come in a hurry, and father said he had to wade to over his waist.'

But Bridget was not convinced. She stood there gazing out seawards at the lighthouse.

'I would like to go there,' she said. 'Can't you see a long way from the top room that's all windows, Celestina? I should think you could see to the — what do they call that thing at the top of the world — the north stick, is it?'

Celestina was not very much given to laughing, but this was too funny.

'The North Pole, you mean,' she said. 'Oh no, you couldn't see to *there*, I'm quite sure. Besides, there isn't anything to see like that — not a pole sticking up in the ground — it's just the name of a place. Father's told me all about it. And so did the old man at the lighthouse. Oh, I would like to go there — better than anywhere — just think how strange it must be, all the snow and the ice mountains and everything quite, *quite* still!'

CHAPTER VIII
A NICE PLAN

> 'Up where the world grows cold,
> Under the sharp north star.'
> —*A North Pole Story*.

Biddy stared at Celestina. The little girl's face was quite flushed with excitement.

'Go on,' said Biddy. 'Tell me some more. I never heard about it.'

'It's what they call the arctic regions,' said Celestina. 'The old sailor at the lighthouse has been there. Once he was there in a ship that got fastened into the ice, and they thought they'd never get out again, and they'd scarcely nothing to eat. Oh, it was dreadful; but I did so like to hear about it. And fancy, in the summer it never gets night up there — the sun never goes away; and in the winter it never gets day, the sun doesn't come up at all.'

'How very funny!' said Biddy. 'What makes it like that? Is it the same sun as ours?'

'Oh yes, but I can't quite explain,' said Celestina, looking rather puzzled. 'Father showed it me with the candle and a little round globe we've got, but I'm afraid I couldn't tell you.'

'Could the old man tell it?' asked Biddy. 'I would so like to go to see him. Don't you think we might some day?'

'Perhaps,' said Celestina. 'When the summer comes perhaps your papa would take you in a boat. Lots of ladies go out to the lighthouse in the summer. It's too cold in a boat in winter.'

'But I don't mean in a boat,' said Bridget; 'I mean walking. I'm quite *sure* we could jump over the little bit of water if we gave a great big jump. I once jumped over a whole brook at grandmamma's — I did really.'

'It's much bigger than that — it is indeed. You don't understand,' said Celestina. 'If you'd ask your papa he'd tell you, I daresay. But I think we must be going home now. I'm sure it's time.'

'I'm sure it isn't,' said Biddy crossly. 'We haven't talked about the dolls at all yet, and I want you to tell me more about that funny place where the snow is.'

'I'll try to think of more to tell you if your mamma will let you go out with me another time, and I'd like dearly to show you my dolls' room if you could come to our house one day,' said Celestina. 'But we must go home now, Miss Biddy.'

Bridget flounced about, looking very much put out.

'I'm not going yet. I don't want to go in,' she said.

Celestina began to look troubled. Then her face cleared.

'*I* must go home,' she said, 'whether you do or not. I wouldn't for anything have mother worrying about me. You wouldn't like your mamma to be worrying about you, would you, Miss Biddy?'

'I daresay she wouldn't care; I'd only get a scolding, and I don't mind much,' said Biddy, who had got on to a very high horse by this time.

Celestina stopped short and looked at her. She could not understand Biddy at all.

'Mother never scolds me, but I'm very unhappy when she's not pleased with me,' she said gently; 'and I'm sure your mamma's very kind and good. I'm sure she does care about you a great deal.'

Her words reminded Bridget of what had happened that very afternoon. Perhaps what Celestina said was true: mamma had pressed her hand when she said she was sorry. With one of the quick changes of mood which seemed so strange to Celestina she turned suddenly.

'I'll go home,' she said. 'Come on, Celestina, before I get naughty again. But it isn't all for being good. It's a great deal that I want to come out with you again, and perhaps I mightn't if I was late today.'

'No. Very likely your mamma would think I made you disobedient,' Celestina replied; 'and I shouldn't like her to think so.'

'If I might go into the kitchen and get the tea ready for papa and mamma like you do, I'd never want to stay out late,' said Bridget thoughtfully.

Celestina considered.

'You don't need to do that,' she said. 'It wouldn't be any good to your mamma, for she's got servants to do it. But there must be other things you could do if you want to help her.'

'No,' said Biddy, shaking her head, 'there's nothing. And I don't think I want very much; it's just sometimes. Alie helps mamma because she's the eldest.'

Celestina scarcely knew how to answer this, though she felt there was something wrong about her little companion's way of looking at things. But Celestina had not much power of putting her thoughts and feelings into words. Her solitary life had made her a very silent child, not intentionally, but by habit. She found it difficult to express her meaning even to herself. Just now she gazed at Biddy without speaking, so that Biddy began to laugh.

'What are you looking at me so for?' asked the younger child.

'I don't know,' said Celestina. 'I was only thinking.'

'What?' asked Biddy again.

'You should help too, even though you're the youngest,' said Celestina bluntly.

'Oh, bother,' was all Biddy's reply.

They were at the Rectory gate by this time.

'Good-bye, Miss Biddy,' said Celestina. 'I must run home fast. But I don't think it's late.'

'Good-bye,' said Biddy. 'I've got my shells; have you got yours? Oh yes,' as Celestina held up a tiny little basket she was carrying. 'How dreadfully careful you are! Good-night. I'll ask mamma to let me come and see you very soon.'

On her way up the short drive to the house Bridget came face to face with Randolph.

'Oh, you're there, are you?' he said. 'Mamma was just asking if you'd come in, so I came to look out for you.'

Biddy was silent. This did not seem very like mamma's 'not caring,' as she had been saying to Celestina.

'It isn't late,' she remarked at last. 'Mamma said I might stay half an hour.'

'She was beginning to worry about you a little, all the same,' said Rough. 'Were you with the little Fairchild girl?'

'Yes,' said Biddy.

'Is she a nice little girl?' asked Rough.

'Yes,' said Biddy again.

'Then why don't you like her? Why are you so cross?' asked her brother.

'I'm not cross, and I never said I didn't like her,' replied Bridget impatiently.

Rough began to whistle.

'I can't say I agree with you,' he said. 'Well, I'll run on and tell mamma you're all right;' and off he set.

Biddy followed him slowly, feeling rather depressed.

'I didn't mean to be cross,' she said to herself in her usual way, though she really did feel what she said this time. 'It was kind of Roughie to come to meet me. They're all good 'acept me. Celestina's good too. I'm made all the wrong way,' and she sighed deeply.

She brightened up again, however, when she met her mother at the door.

'That's right, Biddy dear,' said Mrs. Vane. 'You've not stayed too late.'

Rough was there too; he had not told about her being cross evidently, and Biddy felt grateful to him. It was very nice when mamma spoke like that; it reminded her of the way her hand had been pressed that afternoon. But a sudden thought rather chilled her satisfaction. Biddy was beginning to be troubled with thoughts, and thoughts too that would not be driven away and forgotten, as she had been accustomed to drive away and forget anything that made her feel at all uncomfortable. This thought teased and pricked her for a few seconds, and though she wriggled herself about and stamped her feet down with hard thumps on the gravel, it would not go.

'Biddy,' it said, 'Biddy, you know what you should do.'

So that at last, in sheer impatience of its teasing, she gave her mother's sleeve a little tug.

'Mamma,' she said, 'it was *her* that made me not stay longer than you'd said. I wanted to. I wasn't very good, but she's good.'

Mrs. Vane turned with real pleasure in her face.

'I'm very glad you've told me, Biddy,' she said. 'Yes, it was nice and good of Celestina to remind you. I think she must really be a very conscientious child.'

'I don't know what that is,' said Bridget. 'At least, p'raps I do know, but it's such a trouble to think. But Celestina *is* good. I almost think she's a little too good.'

Her tone was very melancholy. Rough burst out laughing, but Mrs. Vane looked rather disappointed.

'It will be so vexing if Biddy takes a dislike to her just when I was hoping it would be a good thing,' she thought to herself.

Still, the remembrance of the little talk with Mrs. Fairchild was in her mind. She took no notice of Biddy's remark, only telling her cheerfully to run in quickly and get ready for tea, as it was almost ready.

The children's mother went to Seacove again the next day, but this time she did not take either of them with her. She went straight to Pier Street, and as soon as Mrs. Fairchild saw her coming into the shop she came forward with a smile and showed her into the parlour. There Celestina was sitting quietly working at some new clothes for her little dolls: she wanted them to be very smart indeed, in case the Rectory young ladies came to see them. She rose from her seat at once when Mrs. Vane came in, but a shadow of disappointment crossed her face when she saw that the lady was alone.

'I have not brought Biddy this time,' said Mrs. Vane kindly. 'I have come to see Mrs. Fairchild myself. But Biddy shall come some day soon. I want you to show her your doll-house, for I should be glad for her to get into the way of playing with one. She has always been a difficult child to amuse,' she went on; 'she is so restless, and never seems to get interested in her toys or games.'

Celestina opened her lips as if she were going to speak, but said nothing.

'What is it, my dear?' said Mrs. Vane, seeing the look in the little girl's eyes. Celestina grew pink.

'It was only,' she began. 'It's not so nice to play alone.'

'No, that is true,' said Biddy's mother, 'and true of other things as well as play.' Then she turned to Mrs. Fairchild: 'Have you been able to — ' she was beginning, but with a little gesture of apology Mrs. Fairchild glanced at her daughter.

'Go upstairs, Celestina, for a few minutes,' and in a moment

Celestina gathered together her small concerns and noiselessly left the room.

'How obedient she is,' said Mrs. Vane with a little sigh. 'I should have had quite an argument with Biddy, or at least cross looks.'

'Children are very different,' said Mrs. Fairchild. 'Still there is not much you can do with them without obedience. And if they get the habit of it quite young, it costs them so much less; they obey almost without thinking about it.'

'And have you seen Miss Neale?' asked Mrs. Vane after a little pause.

'She came to see me yesterday, and I think it can be nicely arranged. She is a very good girl: I feel sure you will be pleased with her. The only difficulty would have been her promise about Celestina, which she would not have liked to give up; but what you have so kindly proposed puts this all right of course. It will be a great pleasure and interest to Celestina to learn with a companion. I feel that I cannot thank you enough.'

'On the contrary,' said Mrs. Vane, 'I have to thank you. I am in hopes that your little daughter's companionship will be of great good to Bridget.'

Mrs. Fairchild's gentle face grew a little red.

'I think I may at least assure you of this,' she said, 'little Miss Bridget will learn no harm from Celestina.'

'I am sure of it,' said Mrs. Vane warmly. 'By the bye,' she added, 'Celestina is a very uncommon name. I have never heard it except in its French form of "Célestine."'

'Celestina was named after a French lady,' said Mrs. Fairchild — 'a lady who was very kind to my sisters and me when we were young. She happened to be living near the town where our home was for some years. Her husband had an appointment there. They had only one child, a daughter named Célestine like her mother, who died, and my mother helped to nurse her in her last illness, which made Madame d'Ermont very fond of her. Indeed, I think she was very fond of us all,' she added with a little smile, 'and I think I was a special pet of hers. Through her kindness I had many advantages in my education. But when she and

Monsieur, as we always called him, went back to France troublous times came on. We lost sight of them altogether. Still, I have never forgotten the dear lady, and I determined to give my little girl her name.'

Mrs. Vane listened with the greatest interest.

'"Madame d'Ermont," did you say?' she asked eagerly, and on Mrs. Fairchild's answering 'Yes' — 'It must be the same,' she went on; 'our Madame d'Ermont's name was Célestine too. She was, or is, for I hope she is still living, a great friend of ours too, Mrs. Fairchild. We spent two winters in the south of France near her home, and we saw a great deal of her. It is a pity for you not to have kept up writing to her; she is very kind and very rich and childless — she might be a good friend to her little name-daughter.'

Mrs. Fairchild's face flushed again: I rather think Biddy had inherited something of her habit of hasty speech from her mother, kind-hearted and good as Mrs. Vane was.

'It would not be from any motive of *that* kind I should like to hear from Madame d'Ermont again,' said Celestina's mother. 'It is true our child has no one to look to but ourselves, and neither her father nor I can boast of very strong health — but still — '

'Oh, I *beg* your pardon,' interrupted Mrs. Vane impulsively; 'I quite understand your feeling, and I did not mean to say anything you could dislike. But still I will look out Madame d'Ermont's address, or get it from my mother, and when I write to her I may tell her of you, may I not?'

'I should be very grateful if you would do so,' Mrs. Fairchild replied.

Then they went on to speak of the details of the arrangement they had been making, and soon after Mrs. Vane left.

That afternoon she called Bridget to her.

'Bride,' she said, 'I have something to say to you.'

'Yes, mamma,' Biddy replied, but without giving much attention. It was probably, she thought, only to reprove her for her way of sitting at table, or for having been cross to Jane, or for one of the hundred and one little misdemeanours she was always being guilty of. And Biddy was in a queerish mood just now: there was a good deal of battling and pulling two ways going on in her baby heart. Was the lazy little *soul* beginning to grow, I wonder?

'Yes, mamma,' she said indifferently, with her peevish 'I didn't mean,' quite ready to trot out on the smallest provocation.

'You must give your attention, my dear,' said Mrs. Vane; 'it is something rather particular I want to tell you about.'

'I *am* giving my attention,' said Biddy, though it did not look very like it.

'Well, then,' her mother went on, determined not to notice Bride's evident wish to pick a quarrel, 'listen. You know that Miss Millet cannot come back to us for a good long while. Alie's lessons do not matter so much as yours, for she is very well on for her age and a little rest will do her no harm; besides, she will have some lessons with papa and some with me. But we have not time for you too.'

'And you couldn't manage me if you had,' said Biddy gloomily.

Mrs. Vane took no notice — 'And besides, at your age it is most important to be very regular. So I have engaged a daily governess for you, my dear Biddy — that means a governess who will come every morning for three hours, just to teach you. But she won't live in the house with us as Miss Millet does.'

'Won't she take us walks?' demanded Biddy.

'Not every day, for some days she is engaged in the afternoons. But twice a week she will come back in the afternoons and take you a walk and stay to have tea with you. Her name is Miss Neale; she is very nice, though she is younger and — less experienced than Miss Millet. I hope you will be very good with her, Bride.'

Bride gave herself a little shake.

'No, mamma,' she said. 'I don't want to be naughty, but I can't help it. I'm sure I shall be very naughty with her.'

Mrs. Vane kept her patience. She looked at Biddy quietly.

'Why, Biddy?' she asked. 'You are old enough to understand that I have taken a good deal of trouble about this for you.'

'I needn't have lessons till Miss Millet comes back; I'd be quite good without. I don't like having lessons quite alone without Alie or nobody,' said Biddy.

'Would you like it better if you had some one to learn with

you — some one nearer your age than Alie, who would do the very same lessons?' asked her mother.

Biddy's eyes sparkled.

'I should think I would,' she said, 'but there isn't nobody' — then she gave a sort of gasp. 'Oh, if only — if Celestina could do lessons with me,' she exclaimed. 'She knows lots, mamma, all about up at the top of the world, where there isn't *really* that stick I thought there was, but lots of snow and always light — no, always dark, I forget which. I'll ask her — the old lighthouse man told her. I'm sure she'd help me with my jography, mamma, and she'd teach me to dress dolls and — ' Biddy stopped, quite out of breath.

Mrs. Vane smiled; she looked very pleased.

'I am very glad you have thought of it yourself, Biddy,' she said, 'for it is the very thing I have planned. Celestina *is* going to have lessons with you. Her mother had already settled for Miss Neale to give her lessons, as they don't care about Celestina going to school, so it would not have been fair for Miss Neale to give her up to come to us. And besides, both papa and I thought it would make our little girl happier to have a companion — eh, Biddy?'

Mrs. Vane had hardly time to finish her sentence before she felt her breath nearly taken away by a pair of fat little arms hugging her so tightly that she could scarcely free her head.

'Mamma, mamma,' cried Biddy, 'I love you, I do really love you now. I never thought I did so much. Oh, I am so glad. Thank you, dear mamma.'

Never in her life had Biddy been so affectionate; never, at least, had she shown her affection so much. Mrs. Vane kissed her warmly.

'I am very pleased too, dear,' she said. 'I do think you will be a good and happy little girl now.'

'I'll try to be good, mamma, I will really. But it would take me a dreadfully long time to be as good as Celestina, I'm afraid.'

CHAPTER IX
A SECRET

'If the sun could tell us half
That he hears and sees,
Sometimes he would make us laugh,
Sometimes make us cry.'
  —Christina Rossetti.

'You must eat your breakfast properly, Celestina, my dear,' said Mrs. Fairchild to her little daughter one morning in the following week. 'You will be quite faint and tired before dinner-time if you don't, and that would be a bad beginning.'

Celestina on this set to work once more on her bread and milk. She was too excited to feel hungry; her pale cheeks had each a bright spot of colour and her eyes were shining. It was the day on which she was to begin her lessons at the Rectory. Miss Neale was to call for her on her way there, and though she had three-quarters of an hour to wait till Miss Neale came, the little girl was sure she would not be ready in time.

'I never saw her so taken up with anything before,' said her mother; and Mr. Fairchild, who was sometimes disposed to take rather a gloomy view of things, said he hoped they should not regret having agreed to the arrangement, and that it would not lead to disappointment, on which Mrs. Fairchild set to work, as she always did, to cheer him up.

'It will give Celestina a little experience,' she said; 'and even if there should be a little disappointment mixed up with it in any way, it will do her no harm, and Celestina is a reasonable child.'

She was very quiet but very happy as she set off with Miss Neale. It was a bright pleasant morning, 'quite spring-like,' said the young governess, and a walk at that early hour was of itself a pleasure to Celestina. She had not been inside the Rectory since the Vane family had replaced old Dr. Bunton and his wife, and scarcely was the door open when the little girl noticed a difference. The old, heavy, stuffy furniture was gone, and though it was still plain, the house looked lighter and brighter. The schoolroom was a nice little room looking towards the sea; there was a good strong table with a black oil-cloth cover and four hair-seated chairs, such as were much used at that time. But there were two or three pretty pictures on the walls, and a cottage piano, and in the bookcase were a few bright-coloured tempting volumes as well as the graver-looking school-books. Everything was very neat, and there was a bright fire burning, and in a pot on the window-sill a geranium was growing and evidently flourishing. To Celestina it was a perfect picture of a schoolroom, and she looked round with the greatest interest as she took off her hat and jacket, according to Miss Neale's directions, and hung them on a peg on the door.

'You must be very neat here, you know, my dear,' she said; to which Celestina meekly replied, 'Oh yes,' quite agreeing with Miss Neale.

In a moment or two the door burst open and in came Biddy. A very pleasant-looking Biddy, with a spotlessly clean apron, tidy hair, and smiling face, and just behind her appeared her mother.

'Good-morning, Miss Neale,' said Mrs. Vane. 'Here is Bridget, whom, you have not seen before. Good-morning, Celestina. I hope you will be two very happy and good little girls, and that Miss Neale will have no trouble with you.'

Then she went on to explain a little about the books Biddy used, saying that Rosalys would look out any that might possibly be missing, and after telling Miss Neale to keep up a good fire and one or two other small directions of the kind, she left the school-room.

Everything went on most smoothly. Miss Neale could hardly believe that Bridget was the child she had been warned that she would find 'tiresome and trying and requiring great patience.' For, for once Biddy really did her best. She was interested in finding out how much Celestina knew 'compared with me,' and anxious that neither her little friend nor her new teacher should think her stupid or backward. And though Celestina's habits of steady attention had made her memory better and her knowledge more thorough than Biddy's, still Miss Neale could hardly feel that either of her pupils was more satisfactory than the other; both were so obedient and attentive and intelligent.

So the morning passed delightfully.

'And won't it be nice?' said Biddy, as she stood at the gate, whither she had accompanied Miss Neale and Celestina on their way home; 'the day after to-morrow Miss Neale will come back to take us a walk in the afternoon, and you may come too, mamma says, and stay to tea if your mamma will let you.'

How Celestina's eyes sparkled! To be invited to tea at the Rectory seemed to her far more enchanting than if she had received an invitation from the Queen of the Fairies to be present at one of her grandest festivals. She was *so* delighted that she forgot to speak, and Miss Neale had to answer for her, and say that she would not forget to ask Mrs. Fairchild's consent.

'And some day, Celestina,' Biddy went on, 'I want you to ask your mamma to ask *me* to tea, for I want to see your dolls.'

Celestina looked rather grave.

'I'll ask mother,' she said, but there was a little hesitation in her manner. This did not come from any false shame — Celestina did not know what false shame was — but from very serious doubts as to what her father and mother would think of it. She had never had any friend to tea in her life; father was always tired in the evening, and she was far from sure that a chattering child like Biddy would not annoy him and make his head ache. So poor Celestina was rather silent and grave on the way home; Biddy's thoughtless proposal had taken the edge off her happiness.

On her way back to the house Bridget met Rosalys.

'Well,' said Alie, 'and how did you get on, Biddy? How do you like your new governess?'

'*Ever* so much better than Miss Millet,' Biddy replied. Her superhuman exertions had somewhat tired her; she felt rather cross now, and half inclined to quarrel. She knew that Alie was particularly fond of Miss Millet, and she glanced at her curiously as she made her speech. But Alie was a wise little woman.

'I'm so glad,' she said. 'So glad you like Miss Neale, I mean. Of course I knew you'd like Celestina.'

'I don't like her so very much as all that,' said Biddy contradictorily. 'I like her well enough to do lessons with, but she's not very nice about my going there to tea.'

'Going there to tea,' Alie repeated. 'What do you mean, Biddy?'

'Mean what I say. She's coming here to tea two times every week if it's fine, so I think they might 'avite me sometimes, and when I said to her just now I'd like to come, she looked quite funny and only said she'd ask her mother. Not a bit as if she'd like it.'

Rosalys felt very vexed.

'Really, Biddy, you might know how to behave,' she said. 'People don't offer themselves to other people like that.'

'They do,' Bride retorted. 'I've heard papa say he was going to "offer himself to luncheon" to Aunt Mary's, and — '

'She's a relation,' Alie interrupted.

'Well, and once mamma offered herself to tea to old Lady Butler — I know she did — just before we went away at Christmas.'

'That's quite different; she knows old Lady Butler so well — and — and — mamma's grown up and knows what's right, and you're a little girl, and you shouldn't do things like that without asking leave,' said Rosalys decidedly.

'You're a cross unkind thing,' said Biddy; 'and if you speak like that I'll not go on being good any more.'

Then she turned away from her sister and ran down a side-path of the garden, leaving Rosalys looking after her in distress, and half inclined to blame herself for having spoken sharply to Biddy. 'It will vex mamma so if this new plan doesn't do,' she thought regretfully. 'But perhaps Biddy will be good again when she comes in.'

The path down which the little girl had run led to a low wall from which you overlooked the sea. The tide was in, and though at some little distance from the Rectory, Biddy could clearly see the water shining in the morning sunshine, which was yellower and richer in colour now, for the season was getting on; the cold thin wintry look was giving place in this sheltered spot to the warmer feeling of spring. The little waves came lapping in softly; by listening intently and fancying a little, Biddy could almost hear the delicate sound they made as they kissed the shore.

'I wish it was warm enough to bathe,' thought Biddy. 'But if it was *they'd* be sure to say I mustn't, or that I was naughty or something,' and in her anger at the imaginary cruelty of 'they,' she kicked the little stones of the gravel at her feet as if it was their fault! But the little stones were too meek to complain, and Biddy got tired of kicking them, and seating herself astride on the wall, sat staring out at the sea. Somehow it reminded her of her good resolutions, though it was a quite different-looking sea from the evening tide, with the red sun sinking below the horizon, like that first time on the shore.

What a pity it was that she had spoilt the fresh beginning of being so nice and good at her new lessons by being cross to Alie! And in her heart Biddy knew that her sister had not blamed her without reason — it was her old fault of heedlessness; she *was* quite old enough to understand that she should not have asked Celestina to invite her, and she knew too that Celestina had been right in answering as she did. But all these 'knowings in her heart' did not make Biddy feel more amiable.

'It's no good trying,' she said to herself as she got slowly down off the wall — Bridget was always deliberate in her movements — 'I'll just not bother. I'll do my lessons, 'cos I don't want them to say I'm stupid, but I'm not going to try not to be cross and all that. I'm tired of trying.'

Mrs. Vane noticed at luncheon that Biddy was quiet and silent and not particularly amiable looking, but Alie whispered that it had nothing to do with lessons, which had gone off well.

'Don't notice her, mamma; it was only that she was vexed with me for something,' Alie added; so nothing was said to Biddy, and she was allowed to nurse her grievances in silence.

She cheered up a little by tea-time, and told Randolph triumphantly that she had done all her lessons for Miss Neale 'by myself, without asking that nasty cross Alie or nobody to help me.' But she remained very surly to her sister, though Alie tried to prevent her father and mother noticing it.

Next day was rainy and blowy. Miss Neale and Celestina arrived smothered up in waterproofs and goloshes, and there was quite a bustle to get them unpacked from their wrappings and warmed at the schoolroom fire. Biddy made herself very important, and forgot for the time about being vexed with Rosalys.

Lessons went off well, thanks to Bridget's putting a good deal of control on herself, though there *were* moments that morning which made the young governess say to herself that she could understand its being *sometimes* true that Biddy was tiresome and trying. When Celestina was putting on her hat and jacket to go she gave Biddy a little touch on the arm.

'I asked mother,' she whispered, 'about what you said, and mother says perhaps some day you would come early in the afternoon, and we could play with the dolls and have tea for ourselves out of mother's toy cups that she had when she was a little girl. They are so pretty. It wouldn't be quite a real tea, for we don't have real tea till past five, but I'm sure mother would get us some little cakes, and we might make it a sort of a feast.'

Biddy's eyes sparkled.

'Oh, that would be nice,' she exclaimed. 'Yes, please, tell your mother I'd like to come very much. And just fancy, Celestina, that horrid Alie said it was very rude of me to have asked you to ask me. I'm sure it wasn't, now, was it?'

Celestina grew red and hesitated.

'I'm sure you didn't mean to be rude, Miss Biddy,' she said. 'Mother said — ' but here she stopped.

'What did she say?' demanded Biddy.

'I didn't mean to say that she said anything,' poor Celestina answered, 'only when you asked me — '

'*What* did she say?' Biddy repeated, stamping her foot.

'She didn't say you were rude; she said you were only a child,' Celestina answered quietly. Biddy's temper somehow calmed her. 'And I think so too,' she added.

'Then, *I* think you're very, very unkind, and I'll never come to your house at all,' said Biddy.

And thus ended the second morning.

Bridget was a queer child. By the next day she seemed to have forgotten all about it. She was just as usual with Rosalys, and met Celestina quite graciously. But it was not that she was ashamed of her temper or anxious to make amends for it. It was there still quite ready to break out again. But she was lazy, and very often she seemed to give in when it was really that keeping up any quarrel was too much trouble to her. I think, however, that Celestina's perfect gentleness did make her a little ashamed.

Lessons were on the whole satisfactory. Celestina worked so steadily that she would soon have left Biddy behind had Biddy been as idle as had often been the case under Miss Millet. And Mrs. Vane was pleased to think that the plan had turned out so well.

One day, about a week after Miss Neale had begun to teach the children, just as they were finishing lessons, Rosalys made her appearance in the schoolroom. It was one of the days on which Miss Neale and Celestina came back in the afternoon to take the girls a walk and to stay to tea afterwards. Rosalys looked pleased and eager.

'Celestina,' she said, 'mamma has a little message for you. Please come into the drawing-room before you go home this morning.'

Up started Biddy.

'What is it, Alie? Do tell me. Mayn't I come into the drawing-room with Celestina?'

Alie shook her head, though smilingly.

'No,' she said; 'it's something quite private for Celestina.'

'I'll come,' said the little girl, but Bridget's face darkened.

'It's not fair,' she muttered, as Celestina, after carefully putting her books away, left the room.

'Come now, my dear,' said Miss Neale, not very wisely, perhaps — she scarcely knew Biddy as yet — 'you shouldn't be jealous. It's a very little thing for Celestina to have a message to do for your mamma. Some other time there will be one for you to do, I have no doubt.'

Biddy wriggled impatiently.

'They've no business not to tell me,' she said, taking not the least notice of Miss Neale's words. Then she banged down her books and ran out of the room without saying good-morning to her governess.

Miss Neale did not see anything more of her till she and

Celestina returned that afternoon. It was a lovely day, and so as not to lose any of the pleasant brightness of the afternoon, Mrs. Vane had made the girls get ready early and go a little way down the sandy lane to meet the two coming from Seacove. Bridget was gloomy, but Alie was particularly cheerful, and after a while the younger sister's gloom gave way before the sunshine and the fresh air and Alie's sweetness.

'There they are,' she exclaimed, as two figures came in sight; 'shall we run, Biddy?' and almost without waiting for a reply off she set, Bridget following more slowly.

When she got up to them Celestina and Alie were talking together eagerly. They stopped short as Biddy ran up, but she heard Celestina's last words, 'Mother says she'll be sure to get it by to-morrow or the day after.'

'What are you talking about?' asked Bridget.

Celestina grew red but did not speak. Rosalys turned frankly to her sister —

'It's a message of mamma's we can't tell you about,' she said, 'but you'll know some time.'

Alas, the brightness of the afternoon was over, as far as Biddy was concerned. She turned away scowling.

'Why should you know if I don't?' she said; 'and what business has Celestina to know — she's as little as me nearly?'

'Oh, Biddy,' said Alie reproachfully.

But that was all. She knew that argument or persuasion was lost on her sister once she was started on her hobby-horse, ill-temper. She could only hope that she would forget about it by degrees. And after a while it almost seemed so. They went down to the shore, where it was so bright and pleasant that it did not seem possible for the crossest person in the world to resist the soft yet fresh breeze, the sunshine glancing on the sands, the sparkling water in the distance. And Miss Neale was full of such good ideas. She taught them a new play of trying to walk blindfold, or at least with their eyes shut, in a straight line, which *sounds* very easy, does it not? but is, I assure you, very difficult; then they had a capital game of puss-in-the-corner, though the corners of course were only marks in the sand; and with all this it was time to go home to tea almost before they knew where they were.

'How pretty it must be up in the lighthouse today,' said Celestina as they were turning away.

This was the signal for Bridget's quarrelsomeness again.

'Miss Neale,' she said, shading her eyes from the sun, as she gazed out towards the sea, 'Celestina does talk such nonsense. She says you can't walk over the sands to the lighthouse. Now *can't* you? I can *see* sand all the way.'

Miss Neale was anxious not to contradict Biddy just as she seemed to be coming round again, and she was really not quite sure on the point.

'I can't say, my dear,' she replied. 'It does look as if you could — but still — '

'There now,' said Biddy to Celestina contemptuously, 'Miss Neale's bigger than you, and she thinks you *can;* don't you, Miss Neale?'

'Yes, yes, my dear,' Miss Neale, who was on some little way in front with Alie, replied hastily; 'but come on — what does it matter?'

But Biddy's tone had roused Celestina, gentle as she was.

'I know you *can't*,' she said, 'and whether a big or a little person says you can, I just *know* you can't,' and she turned from Biddy and walked on fast to join the others. Seeing her coming, Rosalys called to her.

'Celestina, I want to ask you something,' and in a moment the two were talking together busily.

'It's only the secret, Biddy,' said Alie laughingly; she did not know of Biddy's new ill-humour. 'You mustn't mind.'

Down came the black curtain thicker and thicker over Bridget's rosy face; firmly she settled herself on her unmanageable steed.

'I don't care,' she said to herself as she trudged along in silence beside Miss Neale; 'they're horrid to me — *horrid*. And I'll be as horrid as I can be to them. But I'll let that nasty Celestina see I'm right and she's wrong. I *will*.'

CHAPTER X

BIDDY'S ESCAPADE

> 'And Dick, though pale as any ghost,
> Had only said to me,
> "We're all right now, old lad."'
> *Author of 'John Halifax.'*

Miss Neale was rather in a hurry to get home that afternoon, so she and Celestina did not linger at the tea-table as they sometimes did. By half-past four they had gone, for on Miss Neale's account tea had been ordered half an hour earlier than usual.

Rosalys disappeared — mamma wanted her, she said. So Bridget was left alone, for Rough had begun school some time ago. He rode over every morning, and got home again about six.

'I wonder if papa is in,' thought Biddy idly, for a moment or two half inclined to see if she might pay him a visit in the study. But then she remembered that he had been out all day, and that he was not expected home till dinner-time. There were not many very poor people at Seacove, but there were a great many young men and boys always about the wharf, and some fishermen and their families living half-way between the little town and a fishing village called Portscale, some way along the coast. At Portscale there was a beautiful old church, and a vicar younger and much more active than Dr. Bunton. Mr. Vane and he had made friends at once, and today they had arranged to visit some of these outlying neighbours together, for even though Mr. Vane was not at all strong and had come to Seacove for a rest, he was far too good and energetic not to do all he possibly could.

Biddy felt very cross when she remembered that her father was out. She strolled to the window; it was still bright and sunny — a sudden thought struck her. She hurried upstairs to the room where her hat and jacket were lying as she had just taken them off — her boots were still on her feet, and in less time than it takes me to tell, for Biddy *could* be quick if she chose, a sturdy little figure might have been seen trotting down the sandy path which led to the shore.

'If they leave me alone I'm forced to amuse myself and do things alone,' she said to herself, as a sort of excuse to her own conscience, which *was* trying, poor thing, to make itself heard, reminding her too that there were plenty of things she could have done comfortably at home in the nursery, where Jane Dodson was not bad company when allowed to talk in her own slow way. There were to-morrow's lessons in the first place — pleasant, easy lessons to do alone, and not too much of them; and there was the kettle-holder she was making for grandmamma's birthday! But no, Biddy refused to listen. She was determined to carry out the wild scheme she had got in her head — 'It *will* be nice to put Celestina down,' she said to herself.

A very few minutes' quick walking, or running rather, for Biddy could run too when she chose, brought her to the end, or the beginning, whichever you like to call it, of the long rough road, so to speak, of stones, stretching far out to sea. Biddy had gone some way along it two or three times when out with the others; it was a very interesting place to walk along, as the outgoing tide left dear little pools, which held all sorts of treasures in the way of seaweed and tiny crabs and jellyfish, besides which, the scrambling over the pools and picking one's way was very exciting, especially when there was a merry party of three or four together. Biddy found it amusing enough even by herself, for some little time, that is to say. But after a while she got rather tired of not being able to walk straight on, and once or twice sharp stones cut and bruised her feet, and she wished she had some one's hand to take to steady her. She was very eager to get to the other end of the tongue, or ridge of stones, for once there she felt sure it would be but easy walking over sand to the lighthouse. For the lighthouse as you will have guessed, was her destination!

'I daresay the sand'll be rather wet,' she thought; 'it must be the wetness that Celestina thought was water, for it shines just like water sometimes. I'll run over it very quick and my boots are thick. What fun it'll be to tell Celestina I've been to the lighthouse all by myself!'

But the stones grew rougher and rougher. The tongue was not really more than half a mile long, but it seemed much more. Several times before she got to the end of it Biddy looked back with a half acknowledged thought that perhaps it would be best to give up the expedition after all — no one need know she had tried it. But behind her by this time the rough stones seemed a dreary way, and in front it did not now look far. She felt as if she *could* not go back, and she had a sort of vague hope that somehow or other the nice old man Celestina had told her of would help her to get home an easier way. Perhaps he would take her round in a boat!

At last she got to the end of the stones, and then, oh joy! there lay before her a beautiful smooth stretch of ripple-marked sand — how delightful it was to run along it, so firm and pleasant it felt to her tired little feet. The lighthouse seemed still a good way off — farther than she had expected, but at first, in the relief of having got off the stones, she almost felt as if she could fly. She did get over the ground pretty quickly for some minutes, and even when she began to go more slowly she kept up a pretty good pace. And at last she saw the queer building — it reminded her a little of an old pigeon-house at grandmamma's, for it was not a very high lighthouse — almost close to her. But, Celestina had spoken truly, between it and her there lay a good-sized piece of water, stretching up to the rocks, or great rough stones round the base of the lighthouse — a sort of lake which evidently was always there, filled up afresh by each visit of the tide.

Bridget gasped. But she was determined enough once she had made up her mind. She went close up to the water; it did not look at all deep and her skirts were very short. Down she sat on the sand, less dry than it looked, and pulled off her shoes and stockings, tying them up into a bundle as she had seen tramps do in the country. Then lifting her frock as high as she could, in she plunged. *Oh*, how cold it was! But the water did not come up very high, not over her knees, though now and then a false step wetted her pretty badly. She was shivering all over, but on she waded, till within a few yards only of the sort of little shore surrounding the lighthouse, when — what was the matter with the sand, what made it seem to go away from her all at once? She plunged about, but on all sides it seemed to be sloping downwards; higher and higher rose the water, till it was above her waist, and still every movement made it rise.

'I'm drowning,' screamed Biddy. 'Oh, help me, help me! Man in the lighthouse, can't you hear me? Oh, oh, oh!'

Biddy fortunately had good lungs and her screams carried well. But the water kept rising, or rather she kept slipping farther down. She was losing her head now, and had not the sense to stand still, and she was partly stupefied by cold. It would have gone badly with her but for — what I must now tell you about.

It was what would be called, I suppose, a curious coincidence, the sort of chance, so to say — though 'chance' is a word without real meaning — that many people think only happens in story-books, in which I do not at all agree, for I have known in real life far stranger coincidences than I ever read of — well, it was by a very fortunate coincidence that that very afternoon Bridget's father happened to be at the lighthouse. He had gone out there by a sudden thought of Mr. Mildmay's, the Portscale clergyman I told you of, who had mentioned in talking that he had not been there for some time.

'And it is a very fine mild day,' he said. 'It doesn't take twenty minutes in a boat. If you don't think it would hurt you, Mr. Vane?'

Mr. Vane was delighted. There was a good deal of the boy about him still; he loved anything in the shape of a bit of fun, and he loved boating. So off the two came, and were most pleasantly welcomed by old Tobias and his second-in-command at the lighthouse. And by another happy chance, just as Biddy began to wade, Mr. Vane had come to the side of the lantern-room looking over in her direction.

'What can that be, moving slowly through that bit of water?' he said to Tobias. 'I am rather near-sighted. Is it a porpoise?'

'Nay, nay, sir, not at this season,' replied the old man; 'besides it's far too shallow for anything like that, though there is a deepish hole near the middle.'

He strolled across to where Mr. Vane was standing as he spoke, and stared out where his visitor pointed to. Then suddenly he flung open one of the glazed doors and stepped on to the round balcony — perhaps that is not the right word to use for a lighthouse, but I do not know any other — outside, followed by Mr.

Vane. Just then Biddy's screams came shrilly through the clear afternoon air, for it was a still day, and out at the lighthouse, when there was no noise of wind and waves, there was certainly nothing else to disturb the silence except perhaps the cry of a sea-gull overhead, or now and then the sound of the fishermen's voices as they passed by in their boats. And just now the waves were a long way out and the winds were off I know not where — all the better for the poor silly child, who, having got herself into this trouble, could do nothing but scream shrilly and yet more shrilly in her terror.

Old Tobias turned and looked at Mr. Vane.

'It's a child, 'pon my soul, it's a child,' he exclaimed, and he sprang inside again and made for the ladder leading downstairs. But quick as he was, his visitor was before him. People talk of the miraculous quickness of a mother's ears; a father's, I think, are sometimes quite as acute, and Bridget's father loved dearly his self-willed, tiresome, queer-tempered little girl. Long before he got to the top of the ladder he knew more than old Tobias, more than any of them — Mr. Mildmay or young Williams, the other lighthouse man — had any idea of. He knew that the voice which had reached him was that of his own Biddy, and before Tobias could give him a hint, or ever a word had been said as to what was best to do, he had pulled off his coat, tossed away his hat, and was up to his waist in the water. For though not *so* deep close round the lighthouse as at the dangerous place where Biddy had lost her head, this salt-water lake even at low tide was never less than two or three feet in depth at the farther side.

'I can swim,' was all Mr. Vane called out to the three hurrying after him. But so could Mr. Mildmay, and so could, of course, Tobias and Williams. And it was not so much the fear of his friend's drowning as the thought of the mischief that might come to him, delicate as he was, from the chill and exposure, that made Mr. Mildmay shout after him, 'Come back, I entreat you, Vane; you are not fit for it,' while he struggled to drag off a very heavy pair of boots he had on — boots he had on purpose for rough shingly walking, but which he knew would weight him terribly in the water.

A touch on his arm made him start. It was Tobias.

'Stop you here, sir,' he said; 'Bill's off, and he's the youngest and spryest,' and sure enough there was Williams already within a few yards of Mr. Vane. 'I don't take it there's much danger of no drownding — and Bill knows the deep part. But it's cold for the gentleman, so delicate as he is — we two had best stay dry and be ready to give 'em a hand when they get in. But it beats me, it do, to think what child could be such a fool as to try to cross that there water — such a thing's ne'er happened before.'

Mr. Mildmay did not like to give in, though he knew there was sense in what Tobias said. He stood hesitating, one boot half off, but there was not long to wait. Soon came a cheery cry from Williams, 'All right, sir, all right,' and in almost less time than it takes to tell it, the two men, half-swimming, half-wading, were seen returning, carrying between them a little dripping figure, with streaming hair, white face, and closed eyes.

It was thus that Biddy paid her long thought-of visit to the lighthouse.

She was not drowned, nor anything approaching to it; she had only once, or twice perhaps, been thoroughly under the water; the whole had in reality passed very quickly, but not so had it seemed to Biddy. Unless you have ever been, or thought yourself in danger of drowning, you could not understand how in such a case seconds seem minutes, and minutes hours; and the ducking and the cold and the terror all combined had made things seem worse than they really were. Bridget was almost quite unconscious by the time her father had got hold of her — perfectly stupefied any way; her clothes were heavy too, and she was at no time a light weight. Altogether it was a very good thing indeed that strong hardy Bill was close behind Mr. Vane, whose powers would not have held out very long. As it was, he was whiter even than Biddy, his teeth chattering with cold and nervous excitement, when at last the whole party found themselves safe in the living-room or kitchen of the lighthouse.

Old Tobias had hot blankets down before the fire and a steaming tumbler of brandy and water ready in no time. Biddy, deposited in front of the grate, sat up and looked about her in a dazed sort of way. She felt as if she were dreaming.

'Biddy,' said her father, 'you must take off the wettest of your things at once.'

Biddy began to finger her garments.

'My frock's the worst,' she said; 'and oh, where's my hat gone?'

'Never mind your hat, child,' said Tobias. 'Here, step this way,' and he led her to a sort of partition in the corner of the room, behind which was his own bed; 'take off your things, my dear, and get into bed with this blanket round you whiles I sees to the gentleman. You'll be none the worse of your drenching: salt water's a deal better for not catching cold. It's the gentleman we must see to. It's the new rector, and a delicate gentleman he is.'

Biddy stared up at him.

'It's my papa,' she said.

It was the old man's turn to stare now.

'Your papa!' he exclaimed. He had never dreamt but that Biddy was a Seacove child, tempted out too far by the fine afternoon — a fisherman's or boatman's daughter. But however curious he was to hear more, he had too much sense to cross-question her just then.

'Get into bed, missie, and get to sleep for a bit, while your things dry.'

Biddy had had her share of weak brandy and water; she had never tasted it before, and it soon sent her to sleep.

Tobias went back to Mr. Vane.

'She's all right, sir. I'd no notion as she was your young lady. Was she awaitin' for you on the sands, or how?'

Mr. Vane shook his head.

'I know no more about it than you,' he said. But he still looked so white and faint that the lighthouse man and the others gave all their attention to getting him warmed and dried, and at last they got him to look a little better, though he declared he could not go to sleep.

'You can stay quiet any way,' said Mr. Mildmay. But Mr. Vane looked up anxiously.

'My wife,' he said. 'She will be getting frightened, not about me merely, but the child.'

'I will take the boat back at once and tell her,' said Mr. Mildmay; 'if Williams can come with me, it won't take long. I'll run up to the Rectory, and then we'll bring another man out to help to row us all back again. I'll bring some wraps too. You think you'll be fit to go home in an hour or so?'

'Certainly,' said Mr. Vane decidedly. 'I could not stay here.'

Mr. Mildmay reached the Rectory to find poor Mrs. Vane in a sad state of fright. Biddy's absence had not been discovered for some time, as Rosalys was busy with her mother, and Rough had not come in from school, and everybody, if they thought about her at all, naturally thought she was with some one else. For a girl of seven or eight should surely be sensible enough to be left to herself for an hour in her own nursery or schoolroom! But once the hue and cry after her began, it really did seem as if there were cause for alarm. Every one had some new idea to suggest, ending by Rough, who, as he came riding in on his pony and heard the news, declared she must be hiding out of mischief.

But no — a very short search dispelled that possibility, and the pony had to be saddled again for Rough to set off as fast as he could to Seacove to inquire if the truant had perhaps followed Celestina home.

'And your father not in yet either,' said Mrs. Vane. 'Oh, Alie, what *can* be the matter? Can something have happened to him that Biddy has heard of, and that has made her run off to him — poor Biddy, she is very fond of papa. But if she has run away out of mischief, Alie — oh, *could* she be such a naughty, naughty girl?'

Mrs. Vane was dreadfully excited. Alie had hard work to keep back her own tears.

'Just as we were *so* happy about the doll-house for her too,' Mrs. Vane went on.

Rosalys gave a little sob.

'I *think* perhaps she's at Celestina's,' she said. But in less time than could have been expected back dashed Rough. No, Biddy was not, had not been at Pier Street, but Celestina and her mother were following him as fast as they could to the Rectory — Celestina had an idea — she would explain it all — but she begged Mrs.

Vane to send down to the shore; the sea was out, and it was still light enough to see any one there a good way off.

A party was at once despatched to the sands, in vain, as we know, for by this time Mr. Mildmay had landed from his boat and was hurrying along to calm Mrs. Vane's anxiety. He arrived there a quarter of an hour or so after Mrs. Fairchild and her daughter, so Celestina had had time to explain the idea which had struck her — we know what it was, and that it was the true one — and to relate to Mrs. Vane all her reasons for imagining it possible that self-willed, obstinate Biddy had set out on her own account to walk to the lighthouse.

So when Mr. Mildmay appeared and told his strange story, his hearers were able to explain what to him and Mr. Vane had seemed a complete mystery.

'How *could* she be so naughty?' Mrs. Vane exclaimed. But Alie touched her gently.

'Only, dear mamma,' she whispered, 'think; she might have been drowned.'

'And so might your father, and as it is, I tremble to think what the consequences may be for him. I do feel as if I could not forgive Bridget,' said Mrs. Vane excitedly.

Mrs. Fairchild was very, very sorry for her, but she was a brave woman. She managed to draw Mrs. Vane aside.

'Dear madam,' she said, 'I do feel for you. But we must be just. Remember the child had no idea of what would be the result of her folly. It was really but a piece of childish folly or naughtiness. And it may be a lesson for all her life; it may be the turning-point for her — if — if only you would — if you can meet her — gently — if nothing is said to harden her.'

'I will try. I promise you I will try,' said Mrs. Vane very softly. 'But oh, Mrs. Fairchild, if it has made my husband ill!' and her voice broke.

'We must hope not — hope and pray,' said Celestina's mother in a low voice.

'And there was something so interesting I wanted to tell you; I had a letter today from Madame d'Ermont — such a nice letter. And now all this has spoilt everything,' went on poor Mrs. Vane.

'Never mind. You will tell me about it another time,' said Mrs. Fairchild soothingly. 'Would it — excuse my suggesting it — would I be in the way if I stayed till they come? I have some experience as to chills and accidents of all sorts — and I would like to see how they are.'

'Oh, thank you,' said Mrs. Vane fervently. 'I should be most grateful. I have no one now with any head about me since my last maid left.'

And Mrs. Fairchild stayed — not that evening only, but all night, sending Celestina home to explain matters to her father.

CHAPTER XI
AND ITS CONSEQUENCES

*'"Love will make the lesson light.
. . . Teach me how to learn it right,"
Through her tears smiled Daisy.'* — Anon.

For Mrs. Vane's troubles came thickly just then. Before night it was evident that both Biddy and her father were not to escape all bad results from the chill and wetting; and the Seacove doctor, who was sent for at once, looked grave, shook his head as he murmured that it was no doubt most unfortunate. He would say nothing decided beyond giving some simple directions till he should see how the patients were the next day. Biddy, after a violent fit of crying, which came on when she found her father could not come 'to say good-night,' and begging, among her sobs, to be forgiven, fell asleep, and slept heavily, to wake again in an hour or two, feverish, restless, and slightly delirious. This, however, was on the whole less alarming, for very little will make a child light-headed, than Mr. Vane's condition. There was no sleep for him, poor man; he was racked with pain and terribly awake — nervously anxious to know the ins and outs of Biddy's escapade, and to soften it as much as possible in her mother's eyes. Mrs. Vane kept her promise of being very gentle with Biddy, and indeed, when in her room, and seeing the poor little thing so ill, it was not difficult to be so. But once away from her, and in sight of her husband's sufferings, the irritation against Biddy grew almost too great to keep down. And Mrs. Vane was not very good at keeping down or keeping in her feelings, and each time she burst out it seemed to make Mr. Vane worse. There was no going to bed for either her or Mrs. Fairchild that night; indeed, what she would have done without Celestina's wise and gentle mother I do not know. It was she who sensibly made the best of it all, soothing Mrs. Vane, who really needed it almost as much as Biddy and her father; and the only snatches of sleep Mr. Vane got were when her soft and pleasant voice had been reading aloud to him.

'I don't know how to thank you,' said Biddy's mother tearfully the next morning early, when she at last persuaded Mrs. Fairchild to lie down a little. 'Can't you stay all day to rest?'

But Mrs. Fairchild shook her head, smiling.

'I must go home,' she said. 'At the latest I must go home by ten o'clock. It will be all right till then. I can trust Celestina to see to her father's breakfast and everything, and there's not much doing in the shop before then. Celestina will have let Miss Neale know not to come.'

'How well you have brought your little girl up — how thoughtful and womanly she is; and to think that she is only a year or two older than Bridget!' said Mrs. Vane sadly.

'It has not been exactly my doing,' Celestina's mother replied. 'I often think the very things I would have wished different for her have been the best training. She has *had* to be helpful and thoughtful; she has had her own duties and share of responsibility almost all her life.'

'Biddy never feels responsible for anything — not even for learning her lessons or being ready for meals,' said her mother.

'Well, that is just what wants awaking in her. This lesson may show her that even a child is responsible, that a child may cause sad trouble. One would rather she had learnt it the other way, but it may be what she needed.'

Mrs. Vane sighed. She wanted to be patient, but she could hardly bring herself to feel that a lesson which was to cost Biddy's father such suffering, nay, even to risk his life perhaps, would not be too dearly bought.

The doctor came, but he was not much more outspoken than the night before. Biddy was to be kept very quiet, the more she could sleep the better; as for Mr. Vane, he *hoped* it would not be rheumatic fever, but it was plain he feared it. And he advised Mrs. Vane to get a trained nurse.

A trying time followed. For some days it seemed almost certain that Mr. Vane was in for rheumatic fever; in the end he just managed to escape it, but he was sadly weakened, and the cough, which had disappeared since his coming to Seacove, began again. It would be weeks before he could leave his room.

And Biddy, too, did not get well as had been expected. She lay there white and silent as if she did not want to get better, only seeming thoroughly to wake up when she asked, as she did at least every two hours, how papa was, and sinking back again when the usual answer came of 'No better,' or 'Very little better.' Her mother was very kind to her, but she could not be much with Biddy, and perhaps it was as well, for it would have been almost impossible for her to hide for long her great unhappiness about Mr. Vane.

Mrs. Fairchild came to the Rectory as often as she could; sometimes she sat with Biddy for an hour or more at a time, but Biddy scarcely spoke, and Celestina's mother was both sorry for her and anxious about her.

'There seems no one able to pay much attention to her,' she said one evening at home; 'poor Mrs. Vane is so taken up, and no wonder, with her husband, and Rosalys is as busy as she can be, helping and seeing to everything.'

There came a little voice from the other side of the table: the Fairchilds were at tea.

'Mother, do you think I might go to see her?' it asked. 'I'd be very quiet.'

'I'll ask,' Mrs. Fairchild answered. 'You might come with me to-morrow and wait outside while I find out if it would do.'

Mrs. Vane had no objection — Biddy was really not ill now, she said. It was just one of her queer ways to lie still and refuse to get up. Perhaps Celestina would make her ashamed of herself. So Celestina was brought upstairs, and tapped gently at the door.

'Come in,' said Bridget, though without looking up. But when the neat little figure came forward, close to the bedside, and she glanced round and saw who it was, a smile came over her face — the first for a long time.

'Celestina!' she exclaimed joyfully. But then the smile died away again, and a red flush covered her cheeks and forehead. 'No,' she said, turning on the other side, 'I don't want to see you. Go away.'

Celestina felt very distressed. But she wanted to do Biddy good, so she put back her own feelings.

'Please don't say that,' she said. 'I'll stay as quiet as anything, but please don't send me away. I've been so wanting to see you.'

There was a slight turning towards her on this, and at last Biddy lifted her head from the pillow a little.

'Did you truly want to see me?' she said.

'Of course I did. I've been very sorry about you being ill,' Celestina replied.

Biddy did not speak. Then Celestina heard a faint sound, and going up a little closer still, she saw that Biddy was crying.

'Dear Miss Biddy,' she whispered. Then a pair of hot little arms, not so fat as they had been, were stretched out and thrown round her neck.

'Will you kiss me, Celestina?' whispered Bridget. 'Do you really love me? If you do, you're the only one. I'm too naughty — I've been too naughty. I've as good as killed papa — I know he's going to die. I heard them saying the first night I'd as good as killed him, though I pretended not to hear. And I've been trying to die myself; I thought p'raps if I prayed a great, great lot to be forgiven, God would forgive me before I died. But I want to die, because I'm so naughty I'm only a trouble. And I *couldn't* live without papa, knowing I'd as good as killed him. Oh, Celestina,' and here the voice grew so low that Celestina could scarcely hear it, 'are you quite sure that papa hasn't died already and they won't tell me?' and Celestina felt her shiver.

'I heard him speaking as I came upstairs,' said Celestina, so quietly that Biddy believed her perfectly; 'the door of his room was open. I think he must be a little better today.'

'Oh,' said Biddy with a gasp, 'I do wonder if he is.'

'And — ' Celestina began, then stopped again, 'I don't think you should talk about trying to die like that,' she said. 'I — I think it would be rather a lazy way of being sorry for what we'd done wrong just to try to die.'

'I suppose it's because I'm lazy then. They all say I'm very lazy,' Biddy replied. 'But I can't help it. I'm not going to try and be good any more. I fixed that before — before that day. It's no use.'

Celestina considered a little.

'I should think,' she said at last — 'I should think you would want to get better to help to take care of your papa and make him better.'

Biddy started at this. It was a new idea.

'Do you think they'd let me?' she said in a half whisper. 'I thought I was too little. Did you ever help to take care of your papa when he was ill? But p'raps he's never been ill?'

'Oh yes, he has,' said Celestina, with a sigh. 'I think he's iller than your papa very often. I do lots of things for him then: I make his tea always, and tidy his room. And sometimes when he's getting better and comes downstairs to the parlour I read aloud to him. For when he's ill, mother has all the more to be in the shop, you know.'

Bridget listened intently. At last —

'Celestina,' she said, 'I do wish I could see papa. It would make me *quite* sure he's alive, you know, for it all seems so muddled in my head since the day I was so naughty. And if he'd forgive me, and if he'd get better, I think, *perhaps*, I'd ask God to make me better too, so that I might make papa's tea and read aloud to him like you do.'

'Perhaps it wouldn't be exactly that,' said Celestina, a little afraid of the responsibility of putting anything into Bridget's head, 'but I'm sure you could do *something*. And why shouldn't you see him? Miss Alie was in his room just now.'

Bridget would have hung her head if she had not been lying down. As it was, she looked ashamed.

'He mustn't get up at all, you know,' she said. 'And one day when they offered me to go to see him, I wouldn't.'

'You wouldn't?' exclaimed Celestina.

'No,' said Biddy; 'I didn't want to see him looking like he did that day.'

'But you'd like to see him now, wouldn't you?'

'Yes,' said Biddy. 'If you were to get me my dressing-gown, Celestina, don't you think I might just run down the passage and the little stair and go to see him? He lies on the sofa in his room, Alie said one day.'

Celestina looked frightened.

'Don't you think you should ask your mamma first?' she said. 'Besides, I thought you were too ill to walk.'

'Oh no,' said Bridget; 'I think I could walk if I tried. But you may go and ask mamma if you like; I'm sure she'll say I may.'

Off flew Celestina. She too felt pretty sure that Mrs. Vane would be pleased to hear of Biddy's wish. But when she got to the room where she had left her mother with Mrs. Vane, they were not there, and Alie, who came in a moment afterwards, said they were walking up and down the garden; if Celestina would go out she would be sure to meet them. 'And mamma will be very pleased to hear that Biddy wants to go to see papa. He has asked for her several times, but he said she wasn't to be forced, not till she felt inclined. Papa *is* so good and patient, and he is really a little bit better today,' said Rosalys brightly.

Upstairs Bridget was eagerly waiting for Celestina's return. She had got out of bed and reached down her dressing-gown for herself, feeling rather surprised at finding how well she could walk; she had found her slippers too, and stood there leaning against the bed, quite ready for her little expedition.

After a while she crept to the door and peeped out. Sounds, cheerful sounds of the usual morning stir in a well-managed house came up the stairs; she heard faint clatter from the kitchen, and now and then a little laugh or a few words of the servants talking together. But no one was about upstairs.

'Papa must be a little better,' thought Bridget, 'else they wouldn't seem like that. I do wish Celestina would come back. I wonder if she's forgotten?'

She edged herself a tiny bit into the passage. It did not seem far, only along by the balusters and down the little stair to papa's room; and just then came a sound which seemed to go straight to Biddy's heart. It was papa's cough — not a very bad one, just his usual little cough. It seemed to waken her up — till now she had felt almost as if in a sort of dream; it was so queer to feel and hear all the house-life going on the same as ever when she had been out of it so long, for ten or twelve days is a long time to a child — but the sound of papa's cough seemed to make everything real, to join the past and the present together again, still more, to touch a spring in Biddy which I think she had scarcely known was there. And without stopping to think any more, off she set, along the passage and down the stair, till she found herself, breathless and rather giddy, but full of eagerness, at her father's door.

It was open, as Celestina had said, and half shy now, Biddy peeped in. He was lying on a couch between the fire and the window; it was a bright spring-like morning — he had a book in his hand, but he did not seem to be reading; he was quite still, his eyes were gazing out to the clear blue sky, and the look in his face was very sweet. Then again came the little cough. That was the signal. In rushed Biddy.

'Papa, dear papa,' she cried, as she half threw herself, half tumbled upon him, for she felt giddy again with moving so fast. 'Dear papa, are you getting better? Please don't die, dear papa, and I *will* try to be good. And oh, please forgive me, and don't say I as good as killed you.'

'My poor little Biddy,' said Mr. Vane, raising himself so as to see her, and drawing her tenderly on to the couch beside him, — 'my poor little Biddy. So you've come to see me at last! And are you getting better, dear?'

'Yes, yes, papa, but please tell me you're not going to die because of me,' and Biddy began to cry, but gently, not in her old way.

Mr. Vane tried to speak, but his cough was troublesome.

'I think I'm a little better, dear,' he said, 'and, please God, I hope to be better yet. And it will be a great help to me if I see you quite well again, and trying to be of use to mamma, Biddy, and to Alie. You can help to nurse me, you know.'

Biddy looked up. The very things Celestina had said!

'Papa!' she said, 'might I really? Would mamma let me? Will everybody forgive me?'

Was it Biddy speaking? Even her father could scarcely believe it.

Just at that moment Mrs. Vane came hurriedly into the room: she had been to Biddy's, on receiving Celestina's message, and finding the bird flown, had naturally taken alarm.

'*Biddy!*' she exclaimed, as she caught sight of the child beside her father, his arm round her, her eager flushed face looking up at him — and her tone was rather anxious and annoyed. But Mr.

Vane glanced at his wife with a little sign which she understood. She came quickly towards them.

'Biddy,' whispered her father, 'here is mamma.'

Bridget's face worked for a moment, then she flung her arms round her mother's neck.

'Mamma, mamma,' she whispered, 'I'm going to try to be good — if only you'll forgive me. I don't want to die if I can be good and help to nurse papa. Mamma, there was something *very* sorry came into my heart when papa got me out of the water and I saw how white he was. But I wouldn't listen to it, and it got hard and horrid. But now it's come again — Celestina began it, and I *will* be good — and *don't* you think God will make papa better?'

I don't think Mrs. Vane had ever kissed Biddy as she kissed her then.

Doctors say that *wishing* to get better has a good deal to do with it. It did seem so in Mr. Vane's case; he was not afraid to die, but he was still young, and it seemed to him that if he were spared to live there were many good and useful things he could do. And he was a happy and cheerful man; he loved being alive, and he loved this beautiful world, and longed to make other people as happy as he was himself. Most of all he loved his wife and children, and his great wish to get well was for their sake more than for any other reason. And never during the several illnesses he had had did he wish *quite* so much to get well as now. For he had a feeling that if he did not recover a sad shadow would be cast over Biddy's life — a shadow that would not grow lighter but darker, he feared, as she came more fully to understand that her folly or childish naughtiness had been the cause of his illness and death.

'It would leave a sore memory in her mother's heart too,' Mr. Vane said to himself, 'however much she tried not to let it come between her and the child.'

And I fear it would have done so.

So Biddy's father did his best to get well. Not by fidgeting and worrying and thinking of nothing but his own symptoms, but by cheerful patience. He obeyed the doctor's orders exactly, and forced himself to believe that the work he would fain have been doing would get done, by God's help, even though *he* might not do it; he kept up his interest in all going on about him, watching with the keenest interest the pretty, shy approaches of the spring from his window; he read as much as he was allowed, and helped Rough with his lessons in the evening, and had a bright smile for everybody at all times.

'I almost feel as if he were too good to live,' said Mrs. Fairchild one evening to Celestina and her father, when she had returned from a visit to the rectory. But this time it was Mr. Fairchild's turn to speak cheerily, for he too had been spending an hour or two with the invalid that day.

'I saw a decided improvement today,' he said. 'I do think Mr. Vane's patience is wonderful, but I have a strong feeling that he is really beginning to gain ground.'

Celestina's eyes sparkled with pleasure, and so did her mother's. The two families had grown very much attached to each other in these few weeks.

'*Won't* they all be happy when he gets well?' said the little girl. 'And oh, mother, isn't dear little Biddy different from what she was? She is so gentle and thoughtful, and she's hardly *never* cross. She does so many little things to help.'

Mrs. Fairchild smiled. In her heart she thought that Celestina had certainly had a hand in this pleasant change, but she would not say so. Children got less praised '*then*-a-days,' as a little friend of mine calls long ago, for their parents were exceedingly afraid of spoiling them, and the thought of taking any credit to herself had never entered the child's mind.

'I do hope,' she went on, 'that Biddy's papa will be nearly quite well by her birthday. It'll come in a month, you know, mother, and the doll-house is almost quite ready. Mrs. Vane has begun working at it again the last few days, and Rosalys and I and Miss Neale have all been helping. It *will* be so lovely, mother,' and Celestina's face lighted up with pleasure quite as great as if it was all for herself.

Truly, selfish people have *no* idea what happiness they miss!

CHAPTER XII
ANOTHER BIRTHDAY

'Rare as is true love, true friendship is still rarer.'
—La Rochefoucauld.

Bridget's birthday came in May — the middle of May. From the time I have told you about in the last chapter Mr. Vane went on getting slowly better; at least he got no worse. But it did seem very slow. At last there came a day on which the doctor gave him leave to go downstairs.

'I want to see what he can do,' the doctor explained. 'At this rate we might go on for months and gain little ground. Perhaps he is stronger than he seems.'

They were all very eager and excited about this great step. It was an 'afternoon' day, as the little girls called those days on which Celestina and Miss Neale came back again, and this afternoon Mrs. Fairchild came with them. Mrs. Vane was thankful to have her at hand in case of any help being needed. And all the children were sent out for a walk, with the promise of finding papa in the drawing-room when they came in again.

But as they were coming home they were met by Rough at the Rectory gate. It was one of his occasional half-days. He ran out to meet them, but he looked rather grave.

'Is papa down? Is he in the drawing-room?' cried Rosalys and Biddy.

'Yes,' said Rough; 'but mamma's been rather frightened about him. He seems so weak. She's sent me for the doctor, and he's there now. So you must not go in to see papa. That's why I came to meet you.'

Alie's face fell and Biddy's grew very red.

'I'm sure *we* shouldn't hurt him,' she said. 'It's all that nasty doctor,' and she almost looked as if she were going to get into one of her old tempers.

Celestina took hold of her hand gently.

'Don't, Biddy dear,' she whispered. 'Perhaps when the doctor goes you'll see him;' which did Bridget far more good than if she had overheard, as she luckily did not, Rough's remark to Alie: 'I don't think *she's* any right to grumble when it's all her doing.'

It was not a kind thing to say, but then Rough's heart was sore and anxious, and when one feels so it is difficult not to be cross and sharp. All their hearts were sore, I think. Children jump on so fast in their minds. Bride and Rough, and Alie too, I daresay, had fancied to themselves that once 'downstairs' again papa would seem directly like himself, and this news was a great disappointment. So the little party went in rather sadly, Miss Neale telling them in a low voice to take off their things and come down to tea in the schoolroom as quietly as possible, Rough, over whom her authority did not extend, stationing himself at the front door to watch for the doctor's departure.

He stayed some time, and when he had gone Mr. Vane asked for the children.

'In a little,' Mrs. Vane answered. Then she turned to Celestina's mother. 'This idea has rather taken my breath away,' she said, but her voice was pretty cheerful.

'I hardly see how it is to be managed,' said Mr. Vane, for once rather despondently.

'We will talk it all over afterwards,' said Mrs. Vane, at a little sign from Celestina's mother; 'and now we will leave you to rest a while.'

'Oh dear, Mrs. Fairchild,' she said, when they were alone in the next room, 'I wonder what we can do. It is dreadful to think of going abroad — to be alone among strangers, and my husband so ill. And then leaving the children. I cannot send them to my mother. Her house is full with my eldest brother's family home from India.'

'I think they would get on very well here,' said Mrs. Fairchild. 'And your own governess will be back in a fortnight. Of course Miss Neale would be too young for such a charge; besides, she cannot leave her mother. And — you must excuse my suggesting it — but is not Madame d'Ermont's home somewhere in the south?'

'To be sure,' exclaimed Mrs. Vane, starting up joyfully; 'how stupid of me not to have thought of it! Thank you so much for reminding me. I have her last letter here. You have written to her yourself, have you not?'

'Yes, indeed. I wrote to thank her very much for her kindness,' said Mrs. Fairchild. 'It may be of the greatest advantage to Celestina some day.'

For I have been so busy with the story of Biddy's escapade and its consequences, that I have put off too long telling of the French lady's kind letter to Mrs. Vane about her old friend Mrs. Fairchild and her little name-daughter Celestina.

'It has touched me very much,' she wrote, 'to find I was still remembered; and if ever I can be of use to little Célestine and her mother I hope she or you will let me know.'

Well, the doctor had ordered Mr. Vane to go abroad, as I daresay you will have guessed.

It was a sad disappointment, just when they had come to Seacove and he seemed so well, and though no one reproached her, Bridget felt that the consequences of her self-will were not to be soon forgotten.

It was all settled very quickly; and from the time it was settled Mr. Vane, 'out of contradiction,' he said laughing, really seemed to improve faster than hitherto. So that he was looking a good deal more like 'a proper papa,' as Alie said, the day he and Mrs. Vane started on their long journey.

'I am so glad you are going to be near that nice old lady,' said Alie, amidst her tears; 'and oh, mamma dear, I will try to do everything you would like.'

'I am sure you will, darling, and it is a great comfort to feel so much happier about Biddy now. You will try to make a nice birthday for her, I know.'

'There'll be the surprise — that's something nice to look forward to. And we may have Celestina as often as we like, mayn't we?'

'As often as her mother can spare her, of course,' Mrs. Vane answered.

Then came Biddy. She was not crying, though she winked her eyes a good deal.

'Mamma, I'll try to be good,' she said bluntly; 'and if papa gets quite well again' — here her voice broke. 'Oh, mamma, if only it was the day for you and papa to come back, and him quite, *quite* well. Mamma, I think I'd never be naughty again.'

This was a great, great deal from Biddy!

That day *did* come, but a good many other days had to pass before it came, and some of these were rather sad and anxious ones. For the first letters from abroad were not as cheerful as Mrs. Vane would have liked to make them for the little party so eagerly awaiting them at Seacove Rectory. Mr. Vane was very tired by the journey, and had it not been for the kindness of Madame d'Ermont, who would not hear of them staying anywhere but in her house, at any rate till he grew stronger, Mrs. Vane said she felt as if she would have lost heart altogether. But after a little things brightened up again. 'Papa really seems to get stronger every day,' she wrote; and on Bridget's birthday morning there came a letter from papa himself, all scented with the sweet violets he had slipped into it — for that was long before the days of parcel posts, by which flowers reach us from the south of France and Italy as fresh as if we had just gathered them in our own gardens — and telling of quite a long walk he had been able to take without feeling too tired. The letter ended up with wishing Biddy a truly happy birthday, and hopes that it might be bright and sunny at Seacove. 'I only wish I could pack up some of the sunshine here to send you,' wrote Mr. Vane, 'for we have enough and to spare of it. But after all, the best sunshine of all is that of happy and contented and loving hearts — is it not, my Biddy?'

There was sunshine of both kinds that day at the Rectory. Celestina came early, almost immediately after breakfast indeed, so as to be present at the great 'surprise.' She was to spend the whole day for once with her friends, which was a great treat, though she saw them regularly once or twice a week when she came to have a French lesson from Miss Millet. Mrs. Vane had arranged this before she left, for little Miss Neale, who now gave Celestina lessons every day at Pier Street, could not teach French, and it was a great pleasure, and help too, to Biddy to have industrious, attentive Celestina still her companion in something.

But today, of course, there was no question of lessons of any kind.

They had breakfast extra early, which some children I know, would not, I fear, consider a treat. Indeed, I once heard of some young people, scarcely to be called children, and by no means overworked young people either, who chose for a holiday pleasure that they should stay in bed for breakfast, and not get up till the middle of the day, which, I must say, I did not at all admire. The great reason for the extra early breakfast on Biddy's birthday was not that the Vane children were so *very* fond of being up betimes, but that Rough wanted to be there at the great scene, and with some difficulty he had got an hour's 'grace' from school that morning.

To begin at the beginning — for I know that when I was a child I liked to be told all about everything — the first pleasure of the day, after the reading of papa's nice letter, was the sight of the breakfast-table. Kind Miss Millet and Alie had dressed it up with cowslips after Biddy had gone to bed the night before, for there were cowslips, and very pretty ones, to be had in some woods a mile or two inland from Seacove. And May birthdays always make one think of cowslips.

The breakfast itself was very nice too — extra nice; for there was no bread and milk for once, but only 'grown-up' things — a tempting dish of ham and eggs, and delicious hot rolls and tea-cakes, and strawberry jam and honey to eat with them as a finish up. And besides the letter from papa — which had *really* come the day before and been kept till this morning, as, in his fear of being too late, Mr. Vane had sent it off rather too soon — there was a neat little packet for Biddy from grandmamma, containing a story-book called *The Christmas Stocking*, and a lovely scarf worked in all kinds of marvellous Eastern colours, 'making one think of the Arabian nights,' as Alie said, from the Indian cousins. So that it was with a sigh of deep content that Biddy sat down to breakfast, knowing that something still more delightful and wonderful was in store.

Celestina arrived before breakfast was quite over, and Rough ran out and brought her into the dining-room, where she had to eat a roll and strawberry jam to refresh her after her early walk.

And then when every one had finished and Rough had said grace, they all set off to the schoolroom.

'Shut your eyes, Biddy,' said Rough. 'I'll lead you in, and mind you don't open them till I tell you.'

There stood Biddy, as quiet as a mouse, though her heart was beating fast, till, after one or two whispered directions — 'That isn't quite straight,' 'Put the chairs by the fire, Celestina,' and so on — came Rough's voice —

'Now, Biddy. Open your eyes.'

And 'open her eyes' she did, though she half shut them again the next minute, and then had to rub them to make sure they were not tricking her. For there in front of her, on the schoolroom table, stood, its two big doors flung wide open, the very nicest, most complete doll-house that, in those days at least, could have been imagined. There were six good-sized rooms: drawing-room, dining-room, two bedrooms, nursery, and kitchen — the last, perhaps, the most fascinating of all, with its little kitchen-range, its rows of brightly shining pots and pans, some black, some tin, and some copper; its dresser and shelves, and charming dinner service, and ever so many other things it would take me a very long time to describe. And the dining-room, with its brown and gold papered walls, and red velvet carpet and little stuffed chairs; and the drawing-room, with sofas covered in dainty chintz and blue carpet and gilt-framed mirrors; and the bedrooms, one white and one pink; and the nursery, with the *sweet* little cradle and rocking-chair and baths and wash-hand stands and I don't know all what — truly it was a very pretty sight. Biddy gasped; she could not speak.

'And only think, Biddy,' said Rosalys; 'it is our own old doll-house done up. The one mamma had herself when she was a little girl, you know. Doesn't that make it all the nicer? You *can't* think how we've all worked at it. We'd begun it before — before papa and you got ill; that was our secret that Celestina and I were always whispering about.'

And in her delight even staid Alie gave two or three jumps up into the air! But as she came down again she felt herself caught round the neck and hugged and squeezed. Oh, how she *was* hugged and squeezed!

And '*Oh*, Alie,' whispered Biddy, 'you are too good to me; for you don't know how naughty I felt about your having a secret.'

'Never mind, never mind. I daresay it was my fault. Mamma says it's very teasing to talk about secrets, but it's all right now, and we are all going to be so happy with the doll-house, aren't we? Now you must kiss Celestina too; you don't know what a lot she's done. She hemmed the sheets of the beds and the table-cloths and ever so many things, and her mamma dressed the dolls — and — oh yes, Roughie papered nearly all the rooms, and — '

But here Rosalys, who seemed to be turning all of a sudden into a regular chatterbox, was interrupted by more huggings and squeezings, as Rough rather objected to much of this sort of thing, and Biddy had still a great deal to spare even after she had bestowed a full share upon Celestina. She quieted down, however, when Miss Millet suggested that unless they set to work to go all over the house and admire all its numberless treasures, it would be getting too late for the nice walk they wanted to have before dinner. But in the midst of the showing everything Celestina made them all laugh by calmly taking a little parcel from her pocket, from which she drew out three or four little dolls, announcing that they were Eleanor and Amy and one or two new ones, all in grand clothes for the occasion, who had come to spend the day with the Rectory doll party.

'You did invite them, Alie, you remember, don't you?' she said, looking a little bit aggrieved. 'They would never have come without being invited.'

'Oh yes, I know I did,' Rosalys replied. 'It was only the funny way you pulled them out of your pocket.'

'And some day, Biddy, mother says, perhaps you'll bring yours to drink tea with mine,' said Celestina, quite pleased again. 'We might pretend that mine were some cousins they had in the country who were not very rich, you know,' she went on simply. 'And I'd make their parlour as smart as I could. I'd try to dress it up with flowers and green, so that it would be like an arbour.'

'Yes,' said Biddy, 'that *would* be nice. And *we* might have tea as well as the dolls, mightn't we, Celestina? You know once you told me about some little cups you have that we might have tea out of.'

'Oh yes,' Celestina replied hospitably, '*of course* we'd have real tea too. Mother would make some cakes and — '

'My dears,' said Miss Millet, 'I think we must be going out. You will have all the rest of the day to play with the doll-house, but it is such a lovely morning, and I think it's always so nice to have a good walk on a holiday.'

The little girls were quite of their governess's opinion, only sorry that Randolph could not make one of the party. He came home, however, in good time in the afternoon, and they all had a very merry tea together.

'What a nice birthday it's been!' said Bride, as she and Alie kissed Celestina, whose mother managed to spare an hour to come to fetch her and at the same time to wish Biddy 'many happy returns.' 'How good of you to dress the dolls for me, Mrs. Fairchild!' she went on. 'I think I shall love the doll-house more and more every day, for, you see, it's full of kind things you've all done for me. And I'm going to keep it *so* neat. Mamma will be quite surprised when she comes home to find how neat I've learnt to be.'

'And only think, Mrs. Fairchild,' added Rosalys; 'do you know that papa and mamma will most likely be home in one month? Just fancy, how nice!'

The 'most likely' came true. One month saw Mr. and Mrs. Vane safe back at Seacove; 'papa' so bright and well, so bronzed and ruddy too, that it was difficult to believe he was the same feeble-looking invalid who had started on his long journey nine weeks before.

It is not often — very seldom, indeed — that I am able to tell my readers 'what became of' the children they have come to know, and sometimes, I hope, to care for in these simple stories. But as it is now many years ago since the Vane family came to Seacove Rectory, and as Randolph and his sisters and Celestina Fairchild have long ago been grown-up people, I can give you another peep of them some eight or ten years after the birthday I have been telling you about.

The curtain rises again on a different scene.

It is a lovely, old-fashioned garden, exquisitely neat and filled with plants and flowers, showing at their best in the bright soft light of a midsummer afternoon. A rectory garden, but not Seacove. Poor Seacove, with its sandy soil and near neighbourhood to the sea, could not have produced the velvety grass of that old bowling-green, now (for we are still speaking of a good many years ago) a croquet-ground, or the luxuriant 'rose hedge' bordering one end. Two girls were walking slowly up and down the wide terrace walk in front of the low windows, talking as they walked. One was tall and slight, with a fair sweet face — a very lovely face, and one that no one loved and admired more heartily than did her younger sister.

'Alie dear, I do hope you've had a happy birthday,' said Bridget — sixteen-years-old Bridget! — for Rosalys was twenty-one today. 'There are some birthdays one should remember more than others. A twenty-first birthday is a *very* particular one, isn't it?'

'Yes indeed, Biddy, it is,' Alie replied. 'I can scarcely believe it. And fancy, in five years more *you* will be twenty-one!'

'I hope I shall go on growing till then,' said Biddy, whose great ambition was to be as tall as her sister. 'Some girls do, don't they? And I have grown a good deal this year. I don't look as stumpy as I did, do I?' and Biddy looked up in her sister's face with a pleasant smile — a smile that showed her pretty white teeth and shone out of her nice brown eyes. She was not lovely like Alie, but she had a dear honest face — though she was still rather freckled, and her dark wavy hair gave her a somewhat gipsy look.

'You aren't a bit stumpy — you're just nice,' said Rosalys, 'though I daresay you will grow some more. Just think what a little roundabout you once were, and how you've grown since then.'

'Yes indeed,' laughed Biddy. 'Talking of birthdays, Alie, do you remember my eighth birthday? The one at Seacove, when papa and mamma were away after his being so ill, and when you all gave me the doll-house — the dear old doll-house; do you know I really sometimes play with it still? I often think of Seacove.'

'So do I,' said Alie. 'Of course I didn't like it *as much* as this, for this garden is so sweet and the country all about here is so beautiful, and then it's so nice to be near grandmamma. But Seacove had a great charm about it too.'

'The sea,' said Biddy — 'the sea and the sunsets,' she went on half dreamily; 'I always think when I see a red sunset — ' but then she stopped. There are some thoughts that one keeps *quite* in one's own mind!

'I always feel grateful to Seacove,' she said after a moment's pause. 'Mamma is quite sure that the three years we lived there did more than anything to make papa strong again. What a blessing it is that he is so well now!'

'And quite able for all his work here, though he could never stand London again,' said Alie. 'I wish Rough had gone into the Church too, Bride — that is to say, I wish *he* had wished it. Then we should have had him somewhere near us, instead of far away in India,' and she gave a little sigh.

'But he's getting on so well — he was just *made* to be a soldier,' said Biddy. 'And papa says it is like that. Some people just *feel* what they're meant to be. And Rough is a great comfort, even though he has to be away — and you know, Alie,' she went on quite gravely, 'I don't think there *could* have been another as good as papa, not in the same way: he's just nearly an angel.' Alie did not disagree. 'And Roughie will be home before your next birthday, you know.'

'I hope so indeed,' said Rosalys.

'Talking about long ago,' went on Bride, to whom eight or nine years were still a *very* 'long ago,' 'reminds me of dear little Celestina. What ages it is since we have heard of her — not since the year her father died, and we were afraid they were left rather badly off. How strange it seems, Alie, doesn't it? that poor Mr. Fairchild should have died and papa got well, when you think how ill papa was and that he seemed quite well then.'

'He was always delicate — Mr. Fairchild, I mean,' said Rosalys. 'But it was very sad; they were so very fond of him. But, Biddy, we have heard of Celestina since then — don't you remember, mamma wrote to tell Madame d'Ermont of their trouble, and she wrote to Mrs. Fairchild inviting them to visit her? They couldn't go — not then — but mamma had another letter, thanking her and telling us where they were going to live. Still all that is a good while ago, and when mamma wrote again her letter was returned.'

'How kind they were to us at Seacove!' said Bridget. 'I would love to see Celestina again — fancy, she must be grown up.'

What I am now going to tell you will seem to some people 'too strange to be true,' but begging these wise people's pardon, I cannot agree with them. Strange things of the kind — coincidences, they are sometimes called — have happened to me myself, too often, for me not to believe that 'there is something in it.' In plain words, I believe that our spirits are sometimes conscious of each other's nearness much sooner than our clumsy bodies are. How very often is one met with the remark, 'Why, we were just speaking of you!' How often does the thought of some distant friend suddenly start into our memories an hour or two before the post brings us a letter penned by the dear far-away fingers!

Something of this kind was what happened now. A young man-servant came out of the house and made his way to where the girls were.

'If you please, miss,' he said, 'a young lady is in the library waiting to see you. My mistress is out. The lady asked for both you and Miss Bridget.'

'Who can it be?' said Rosalys.

'How tiresome!' said Biddy.

But they were accustomed to see visitors that had to be seen when their mother was out, and they went together to the library.

Alie went in first, but she stood perplexed and a little confused as a slight tall figure rose from a chair and came forward to meet her.

'I am afraid,' the stranger began, but before she could say another word, or before Alie had time to do more than think to herself, much more quickly than it takes to tell it, that surely she *should* know that sweet pale face and bright though gentle eyes, Biddy had darted forward and was throwing her arms round the young girl's neck. 'Don't you know her, Alie?' she cried. '*I* do. It's dear little Celestina, grown up, and oh, how nice and pretty and good you look! And we've been speaking of you all this morning. It's Alie's birthday; she's twenty-one, just fancy! And where have you been, and where's your mother, and — '

Her breathlessness gave Rosalys time to come forward and warmly kiss Celestina in her turn. Then they made her sit down; she was looking rather tired, for she had had a long walk in the sun — and by degrees she told them all her news. There was a good deal to tell. The last four years had been spent by her mother and herself in France, not far from Madame d'Ermont, whom Celestina described as having been more than kind.

'She paid for all my schooling and lessons,' the girl said simply, 'so that mother could afford to stay with me all the time. Mother gave some English lessons herself too. And I was able to learn French *quite* well, which will be such an advantage to me. The last two years I taught English at the school, so the expenses were not so great. And we spent the summer holidays at Madame d'Ermont's château. Oh, she was *so* kind!'

'But why have you not written to us all this time?' asked her friends.

'We have — two or three times, but the address must have been wrong, for one letter was returned to us. I remember I put all rightly except the county, for I did not think that necessary; and now — the other day, I mean — when, we had answered the advertisement and were inquiring about Calton, we found that there are actually three or four places of the name in England. And oh, we were so delighted when we found on getting there that Laneverel Rectory was only two miles off.'

'Are you living at Calton then? What do you mean about an advertisement? Is your mother at Calton?'

Celestina laughed and blushed at her own confused way of explaining.

'I am so pleased at seeing you that I am losing my head,' she said. 'Yes, we have come to live at Calton. We have got the dearest little house there. And I am French teacher at the large girls' school just outside the town. I get sixty pounds a year — is it not delightful? So we are quite rich. If only — you don't know how I wish poor father could have enjoyed it too — if he could but have had a few years of the pleasant life and rest.'

She smiled through the tears in her eyes. Biddy stroked her

hand gently.

'But you yourself — it isn't all rest for you?' said Alie, thinking as she spoke that it was 'Celestina all over,' never giving a thought to herself.

'Oh no, I have to work of course. But I like it. And some of my pupils are very nice and intelligent. Besides — I should be miserable if I were idle,' she added brightly.

'Yes, indeed,' both the girls heartily agreed. 'We are very busy too, Celestina. We have lots and lots of things to do at home to help papa and mamma, and all the village people to look after, and the schools and the choir and the church. You must see the church, Celestina.'

'It is just — almost, at least — perfect,' added Biddy enthusiastically, 'compared with poor old Seacove! Oh, do you remember the high pews with curtains round, and the old clerk, and the pulpit like a Queen Elizabeth bedstead.'

'Only *without* curtains,' said Celestina, at which they all laughed. They were so happy they would have laughed at anything!

Then Celestina had to be told about Rough, and how well he was getting on, though so far away, alas! And *then* she had to be taken out into the garden to see its beauties, and have promises of unlimited cuttings and seeds and I don't know all what for her own little garden. There was poor old Smuttie's grave to show her too, in one corner, for Smut had lived to enjoy a year or two of peaceful and slumberous old age on the sunny doorstep in summer and the library hearthrug in winter at Laneverel Rectory. And *then* came the sounds of wheels, and the pony carriage turned in at the gate with Mr. and Mrs. Vane, and all the story of the joyful surprise had to be told over again.

The rector and his wife welcomed their old young friend as heartily as their daughters had done, you may be sure. They pressed her to stay to dinner, promising to drive her home in the cool of the evening, but this, Celestina, unselfish as ever, would not do, for 'mother' might be uneasy. So they had a very delightful 'afternoon tea' in the garden, for afternoon teas were just coming into fashion, and Rosalys and Bride walked half-way home with

Celestina, parting with invitations and promises on both sides. Celestina was to spend at least *half* of her half-holidays at the Rectory, and Alie was to drive to Calton to fetch Mrs. Fairchild the very next Saturday, and the sisters were to pay Celestina a long visit the following week, to see the dear little house and all her treasures.

'You shall have tea in the sweet little French tea-cups Madame d'Ermont gave me,' said she joyfully. 'They are a *little* bigger than my doll ones long ago.'

'Oh dear,' said Biddy, 'that reminds me of the time I invited myself to tea to your house, and Alie was so shocked at me. I *was* a horrid little girl.'

'No, you *weren't*', said both the others. 'And any way,' added Alie fondly, 'isn't she nice now, Celestina?'

'I've never had any friends, if I may call you so,' was Celestina's indirect reply, 'that I have cared for as for you two,' and there was a dewy look in her gentle eyes which said even more than her words.

A *real* friendship — a friendship to last through the changes that *must* come; a friendship too firmly based to be influenced by the fact that none of us, not even the sweetest and truest, are 'perfect,' that we *must* 'bear and forbear,' and gently judge each other while in this world — such friendships are very rare. We are not *bound* to our friends, not obliged to make the best of them, as with relations, and so, too often, we throw each other off hastily, take offence in some foolish way, and the dear old friendship is a thing of the past, one of those 'used to be's' that are so sad to come across in our memory. But it is not always so. Some friendships wear well, sending down their roots ever deeper and more firmly as the years go on, spreading out their gracious branches ever more widely overhead for us to find shelter and rest beneath them in the stormy as in the sunny days of life. And oh, dear children, such friendship is something to thank God for!

My little girls, whose friendship began in the old back parlour at Seacove, are not even young women now — they are getting down into the afternoon of life — but they are still friends, true and tried. Friends whom sorrow and trials only join together still more closely; whose love for and trust in each other even death cannot destroy.

THE END

www.ingramcontent.com/pod-product-compliance
Lightning Source LLC
Chambersburg PA
CBHW031648040426

42453CB00006B/248